Atlantis

from a Geographer's Perspective

Ulf Erlingsson, Ph.D.

Atlantis

from a Geographer's Perspective

–

Mapping the Fairy Land

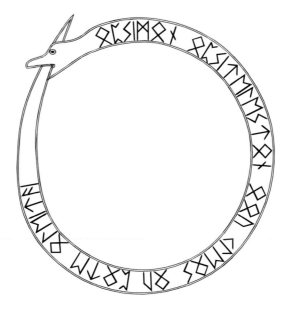

First Printing

Front cover: Achill Island, Ireland. Back cover: Newgrange, Ireland.
Original languages English and Swedish
Printed by Kristianstads Boktryckeri AB, Sweden.
The printshop is ISO 14001 certified. This book is manufactured using only renewable energy.

Published by Lindorm Publishing, Miami Springs, FL, USA
E-mail: orders@lindorm.com   URL: www.lindorm.com

Library of Congress Control Number: 2004094281
ISBN 0-9755946-0-5   Hardcover
ISBN 0-9755946-1-3   Paperback

To Alarik

If you are afraid of dying,

you are not living.

Acknowledgements

incere appreciation goes to my wife Ninotchka, as well as to my parents Erling and Karin, without whose support this work would have been impossible. I am also indebted to a number of colleagues and professors at the university of Uppsala, and—not to forget—to all those teachers, from first grade and up, whose work is so important but who are often overlooked later in life when the rewards of their work is harvested. Furthermore, I am grateful to friends in Greece for assistance with data and logistics. Thanks are also due to all who read the manuscript and suggested improvements. All comments have been appreciatively received and many have contributed to improving the manuscript, albeit sometimes in other ways than the proposer had in mind. Nobody mentioned, nobody forgotten. Finally, thanks are due to those who, long time passing, heaped up a cairn and built a stone cist, in which grave I slept, on the top of the Hill of Auge.

Table of Contents

1. The Location of Atlantis   1
   The Hypothesis
   The Details in Critias
   Testing the Hypothesis
   The Sunken Island

2. Poseidon's Temples   29
   Miosgan Meadhbha
   Boyne Valley
   Brú na Boinne
   Knowth
   Dowth

3. The King's Hill   49
   Tara
   Another Temhair

4. Orichalcum   61
   A Red Substance
   A Paradox
   A Long Shot
   A Final Thought

5. To Think Free is Great   71
   The Neolithic ®evolution
   The American Connection
   Ale's Stones

6. On Myth and Science   87

References   97

Internet Links   98

Indexed Glossary   99

List of Illustrations

Map of Megalith Areas in Europe 9
Map of Ireland 16
Diagram of Island Dimensions 17
Elevation Map of Ireland 18
Pre-historic map of northwestern Europe 22
Depth Map of the North Atlantic Ocean 28
Map of Central Ireland 30
Photo of Queen Maeve's Cairn 31
Photo of Dolmen at Carrowmore 32
Map of Boyne Valley 33
Photo of Newgrange from Dowth 34
Photo of Newgrange's Facade 35
Photo of Newgrange's Entrance 36
Photo the Entrance Stone of Newgrange 37
Plan of Newgrange, with three photos 38
Photo of Knowth 40
Plan and Profile of Knowth, with photo 41
Aerial Photo of Dowth 44
Plan of Dowth 45
Photo Inside Dowth 46
Map of Co. Meath 50
Aerial Photo of Tara 51
Photo of Mound of the Hostages 52
Photo of the Stone of Destiny 53
Photo of the Stone at Turoe 56
Map of Hibernia, based on Ptolemaios' data 57
Thematic Map of the Frequency of Haplogroup X 75
Photo of a Pineapple Plant 76
Aerial Photo of Ale's Stones 82
Plan of Ale's Stones 83

Foreword

T he myth of how Atlantis sank in the sea, and about the culture that disappeared as a result, kindles the fantasy. Often the myth is associated with an early, highly developed culture in the history of humankind. As an information source, myths are hard to interpret, and they leave a lot of latitude for different readings.

In this book, the author uses classical scientific methodology. He erects hypotheses and tests them. Sections of Plato's texts are referred to, and compared to archaeological data and geographical knowledge. The possibility of a documentary content in scriptures that are commonly considered mythological is discussed and analyzed. A series of geographical circumstances indicate that some of these, which commonly are not considered of documentary value, nonetheless coincide well with the geography of Europe, if the changes during the millennia after the Ice Age are considered. We are reminded that large areas in the North Sea and other areas were drowned when the great ice sheets melted, something that a contemporary observer must have experienced as a sinking of the land.

This book highlights how myths can give clues, and that these—read in the right way—can give factual information. Not at least interesting are the parts in which the Irish cultural heritage, from the time we commonly refer to as the Stone Age, is described. Several of these monuments are at least as impressive as some of the classical ancient monuments. Archaeological data on these upwards of 7,000 years old monuments are presented, and their geographic location is compared to the content of preserved myths.

The present book will surely not be the last to discuss the myth of Atlantis. However, being based on geographical and archaeological knowledge, it will probably be deemed one of the most read-worthy.

Professor Wibjörn Karlén

Editor of *Geografiska Annaler Serie A*

Member of the Royal Swedish Academy of Sciences

Author's Preface

It is hard to explain how I got into this situation. Writing about Atlantis, that is. In a way, it started on a cold winter night, Dec. 27, 1996. Sitting on a plane from America to Europe, I fell asleep and had a dream: The standing stones of Ale Stenar, near our home in southern Sweden, were oriented in the direction of the rising sun at midwinter solstice. Waking up from the dream, I looked out through the window, and saw a beautiful full moon over the wing. As I watched it, a bright, shooting star fell right in front of the moon. The feeling was magical at ten kilometres above the moonlit Atlantic Ocean.

Home again, I forgot about the dream. Until one night, about 6 weeks later. Driving home after another night flight I suddenly remembered it, and the impulse to investigate was irresistible. The road took me past the stones around 1 AM, and I stopped. Wrapped in a black blanket from the car, I climbed to the top of the ridge, looking like the grim reaper. It was a bitter cold and somewhat windy night, crystal clear with no moon, but with countless stars. They were twinkling like a spark in the dark eye of an exotic beauty; such as my wife, just pregnant with our first child. The snow had blown off the heath, only an ice cover remained. Sure enough, the stones were oriented exactly in NW–SE, which is the direction of midwinter sunrise (and midsummer sunset) at this latitude. When returning to the car around 2 AM, my eyes caught sight of a large comet just rising over the horizon, with its head pointing at our village. The comet of Hale-Bopp had been all over the news, but since I had been away on a jungle expedition, it was news to me. It was an awesome sight.

Pondering on these and other coincidences, I started wondering why and when Ale Stenar was built, and by whom. Researching archaeology and mythology, I laid the puzzle of the pre-history of Europe. Still, no solid theory for Ale Stenar emerged. It remains an un-solved mystery.

In any case, one day while studying Plato in search of the ancient geography of Athens, I came across the original account of Atlantis. To my surprise, I recognized it. My first instinct was of course to try to prove the idea wrong, so that I could toss it in the round file, and go on reading about Athens. The events that followed is the story of this book.

It is not without hesitation I publish the results, since Atlantis is so controversial. What settled the matter was the realization that there is a genuine demand for a study of this kind, and that researchers are unwilling or unable to satisfy that demand, precisely because it is so controversial. Ultimately it is an ethical question. If not me, who? Sometimes a scientist has to do what a scientist has to do.

1. The Location of Atlantis

A seemingly endless stream of announcements reaches us through the news, with claims that Atlantis has been found. Routinely, other scholars vehemently insist that Plato was just making the whole thing up.

Nobody by his right mind is denying that part of Plato's story about Atlantis is fiction. The question is rather if all of it is false, or if some of it is true. We should not throw out the baby with the bathing water.

This book is an attempt at permanently settling the question of whether the geographic description of Atlantis was based on a real place. The answer is a resounding yes. Beyond reasonable doubt, Plato based the geographic description on Ireland.

However, that does not automatically mean that Ireland politically once was the way Plato described Atlantis. That could be part of the fiction. Extracting the truth from the fiction is a laborious task—if not impossible—around which subsequent chapters speculate.

What are our sources? The complete story about Atlantis is to be found in two dialogues by Plato, written around 360 to 347 BC: *Timaeus* and *Critias*. Plato is the only original source that mentions Atlantis.

Plato's character in the dialogue (Critias, in real life an older relative of his) is supposed to give Socrates a description of an ideal city-state. As point of origin he takes a true story that, so he claims, was told to him by his grandfather, whose father in turn heard it from the famous statesman Solon, who had heard it from Egyptian priests in Sais around 600 BC.

Sais, a city on the western Nile delta in Egypt, was at that time at its zenith as a centre for foreign trade. This was, as you understand, centuries before Alexander the Great established Alexandria. The priests of Sais claimed that their city was founded by the same people as Athens, and had the same goddess, except they called their goddess Neith rather than Athena.

In spite of this common history they naturally had a different language, since Greece later had switched to an Indo-European tongue. The original population of the Aegean region may well have been derived from northernmost Africa—the coast that was then called Libya.

Returning now to Solon's visit in Sais, he was telling the priests about all the oldest myths of Greece, including the one about Deucalion's deluge, when almost all of humankind succumbed. One of the old priests replied in these words (in Benjamin Joett's translation):

-O Solon, Solon, you Hellenes are never anything but children, and there is not an old man among you.
Solon in return asked him what he meant.
-I mean to say, he replied, that in mind you are all young; there is no old opinion handed down among you by ancient tradition, nor any science which is hoary with age. And I will tell you why. There have been, and will be again, many destructions of mankind arising out of many causes; the greatest have been brought about by the

agencies of fire and water, and other lesser ones by innumerable other causes.

Thereafter he said that the myth about Phaëthon was based on a real event, a disaster, even though it now had the form of a myth. In the Greek myth Phaëthon, the son of Helios, wanted to prove that he was the son of the sun, by driving his chariot over the sky one day. However, he could not control the horses; first, he came too high and it got cold on Earth, then he came too low and burnt the land. At that time, his father intervened and destroyed him with a thunderbolt. He crashed in the sea, and his sisters, the Heliads, cried over him. Their tears turned into amber (amber is only found on the shores of the North and Baltic Seas, incidentally).

The priest in Sais told Solon, that this myth is really about a declination of the bodies moving in the heavens around the earth, and a great conflagration of things on the earth, which recurs after long intervals. When it happens, those who live in the mountains or on dry, open places are more exposed, than those who live by rivers or at the shore. Those who lived in Sais had the river Nile for such protection. When, on the other hand, the gods inundate the earth with flash floods, the only survivors in Greece are the shepherds on the mountains, he said, while those who live in the cities, are carried out in the sea by the water. The water in the river Nile rises from below, he continued, and does not come flashing down from above. For that reason the archives of Sais were the oldest.

The explanation of Phaëthon's ride, and the words about natural disasters, can serve as a litmus test. If they reflect genuine knowledge, then parts of the tale may indeed come from Egypt.

Based on my knowledge of geomorphology (the landscapes and the processes that shape them), and from my background of studying natural hazards, my impression is that Plato's text does reveal genuine knowledge of rare natural disasters. Present-day natural hazard fears are typically focused on earthquakes and hurricanes, in a global perspective. However, the truth is, earthquakes rarely kill anyone (it is the poorly constructed housing that is lethal), and in a hurricane, it is the flooding that kills. Finally, meteorites are hardly even on the radar screen today, but they do pose the greatest danger in the very long term, just as Plato wrote. So, that old text contains grains of truth that go beyond even the present-day "conventional wisdom".

Allow me to summarize the natural hazards. Inundations can roughly be divided into flash floods, and floods in which the river overflows its banks. The former occur at or near where it is actually raining, when the water cannot reach the rivers as fast as the rain is falling. The latter may occur far from the rainfall, on the low and flat portions of the river, and are caused by the water being unable to flow out of a stretch of river as fast as it flows into it. Overbank flow of this kind (*desborde* in Spanish) is good for the soil, and the risk of fatalities is small. A flash flood on the other hand is extremely dangerous, and the survival rate of those carried along by one, is low.

Even more dangerous are the mudflows. When thick mountain soils become saturated with water, they may flow away like porridge, similar to the lahars we see every now and then from volcanoes. This has happened in China in the last decades. Deforestation is what makes it possible, and torrential rains—perhaps in combination

4

with earthquakes—are the triggers. Everything on the valley bottom is obliterated, and the flows in China have obtained depths of tens of metres. Massive boulders, the size of houses, are moved along.

As if this was not enough, we have the tsunamis to consider. Submarine earthquakes, volcanic eruptions, or landslides, can set off long-period surface waves (many minutes). When they reach land, they rise in height and may reach far inland. Greece is very seismic, and events such as the explosion of Thera (Santorini), probably in 1159 BC, will surely have wrecked havoc on all harbours in the Eastern Mediterranean. That event was probably the last big disaster before their conversation.

Incidentally, the Latin word "disaster" literally means 'evil star', while the Greek "catastrophe" literally means 'down-bending', 'declination'. The English expression "go under" means 'cease to exist' (the world, for instance), though literally it just means 'travel below'. It appears that all these terms refer to collisions with heavenly bodies. It is also apparent that much of the old mythology—such as the Greek god Zeus, the Nordic god Thor, and the Irish god Manannan—originally may have dealt with these heavenly bodies. A lot of superstition has obfuscated our ability to understand the old tales.

Since Phaëthon's ride already then had the form of a myth, it must refer to a meteorite that fell in the sea well before (many centuries at the least, perhaps millennia) the conversation in Sais. The Kaali crater on the Estonian island Saaremaa (Swedish: Ösel) in the Baltic Sea, is out of the question, since it has been dated to 800 – 400 BC. A possible date would be the meteorite that fell on, and obliterated, a town on the Arabian Peninsula around 2,500 BC. We now know that meteorites may break apart when entering the atmosphere, and fall down in many pieces, just like a certain Columbia. A piece may have fallen in the Aegean Sea, and brought evil destruction to Greece.

The conclusion is that the words by the Sais priest were very sober and truthful so far. It is a bit comical, though, to read that the Greeks are like children with no long tradition, since they are now among the most historically aware. You can buy Strabo in paperback on a subway station of Athens, printed in both the original and in Modern Greek (Strabo is the "father of geography" and lived over 2,000 years ago). While Greece is now preserving the ancient memories, I suppose much of the old Egyptian archives were destroyed with the library of Alexandria. Plundering libraries and museums has devastating effects for civilisation. Then again, perhaps that is why some powers do it? May the verdict over those in charge never die.

Enough said; let us not get tied up in the events of our millennium, but transpose ourselves to classical Athens, when Parthenon was fresh and new, and you would have had to wait for almost two thousand years if you would have ordered coffee at a local café. However, as they say in Greece, if you want good coffee you must have patience.

In this coffee-free environment, you might have been able to hear Plato recite the dialogue, telling you this:

Atlantis was an empire in the Atlantic Ocean, which attacked—un-provoked, in a war of aggression—all of Europe and Asia. In those days, ships could still sail the Atlantic Ocean. Outside of the strait known to the Greeks as the pillars of Heracles, there was an island, bigger than Libya and Asia combined. It was also the way to other islands, and from these one could pass to all of the opposite continent that surrounded the true ocean; because this sea that is within the Straits of Heracles is just a harbour, with a small opening, but the other is the real sea, and the surrounding land can in truth be called a borderless continent.

On the island Atlantis there was an empire by the same name, which had rule over the whole island and several others, and over parts of the continent, and, furthermore, over parts of Libya within the columns of Heracles as far as Egypt, and of Europe as far as Tyrrhenia. In a campaign of war, they tried to subdue Athens, Sais, and the whole area inside the straits. In this war, the Athenians alone stood their ground and defeated the invaders. They thus saved the other peoples from slavery, and liberated all who dwell within the pillars.

However, soon afterwards, violent earthquakes and floods occurred, and in one single day and night all Athenians, in a body, sank into the earth. The island Atlantis disappeared in the same way in the sea. The sea on that spot became impassable and impenetrable, since there was a shoal of mud in the way, caused by the subsidence of the island.

Those are the basic facts. It is already obvious that there are elements in the story that are known to us today, but that were not known to the Greeks in Plato's time—such as the fact that the Atlantic is a true ocean, and that there is another continent on the other side: America; or that there is a chain of islands between them, which constitutes the easiest way for primitive ships to get across. I am of course referring to the route the Vikings took. No leg is longer than a few days on that route, and due to the high latitudes there is not even night sailing involved. Today the area is too stormy for open vessels, but during the climatic optimum that may not have been the case.

If those things were based on facts, then how comes, and what about the rest? The implicit mentioning of America is of course the basic reason why Atlantis has achieved so much attention only now, the last half millennium after the re-discovery of America.

The Hypothesis

The first time that I read Plato's words about the extent of the Atlantic empire—plotting it on my inner map—it occurred to me that the map resembled one that I had recently seen. I tentatively assumed that the places mentioned are those that they traditionally are considered to be. That is, the Atlantic Ocean is the Atlantic Ocean, Athens is Athens, Sais is Sais, etc. It may seem superfluous to mention this, but it never hurts to make oneself aware of ones assumptions. Here is one example why:

Since classical times, the Straits of Heracles has meant the Straits of Gibraltar. However, already the Romans noted, that Germanic inhabitants on the North Sea coast claimed, that the pillars of Heracles actually were to be found in their neck of the woods. Luckily for us, this does not really matter when we are trying to find Atlantis, since the ocean outside the North Sea and outside the Mediterranean Sea is one and the same: The Atlantic.

Thus, the empire had its centre on a large island in the Atlantic Ocean, and it included parts on the European and African continents as far as to Tyrrhenia and Libya. Now, the Tyrrhenoi or Tyrsenoi was an ancient Greek name of the Etruscans, and the Tyrrhenian Sea is

Megalith monuments are found in the grey area. The broken line delineates the extent of the Funnel Beaker Culture, the megalith builders of northern Europe. In Poland, long barrows were built with logs instead of stone slabs. Since this could be due to lack of suitable stones, they might belong to the same tradition. The star marks where the most impressive monuments are found: Co. Meath on Ireland.

still today the name of the sea to the southwest of Italy (the Romans called them Tusci*, after which we now have the province Toscana). Libya in turn, was the ancient name for Africa.

As the map here shows, this pretty well coincides with the extent of the megalith monuments in Europe. They, too, reach almost to Libya in Africa, and to Tyrrhenia in Europe. They, too, cover a large island in the Atlantic, namely Ireland. Furthermore, Ireland has

---

*Although this resembles the Scandinavian word "Tyska", the latter is cognate to "Deutch"; they both come from "Thiudin", which means 'people' (referring to the popular language, as opposed to Latin).

the most impressive of the megalith monuments, along the river Boyne, in Co. Meath.

Having come up with a candidate for Atlantis, the prudent thing to do is to formulate a hypothesis, and then try to prove it wrong. For clarity, I have split the hypothesis in two, one concerning the geographical location, the other concerning the historical timing:

The island Atlantis is Ireland, and
The Atlantic Empire created the megalith culture

Since Plato mentioned that Atlantis was bigger than Libya and Asia combined, and Ireland obviously is not, that merits an explanation. It is quite simple. Size was measured as sailing time, suggested Vinci (1998). In this case, we have to compare the time it takes to circumnavigate Ireland (keeping clear of shoals and beating against the wind being part of the challenge), with sailing straight lines in favourable winds between the harbours in the eastern Mediterranean (since "Libya" and "Asia" just referred to the coastlands).

The Details in Critias

To test the hypothesis we need more data, information that was not used when formulating the hypothesis. We find these details in the second dialogue, Critias.

There was a very fertile plain in the centre of the island, with a view to the sea. Near the plain, and in the centre of the island at a distance of about 50 stadia, there was a mountain, not very steep on any side. In this mountain dwelled one of the earthborn primeval men of that country. His name was Evenor (most names are translated to Greek from Egyptian, according to Plato). With his wife Leucippe, he had a daughter called Cleito.

When her parents had died Poseidon fell in love with her, had intercourse with her, and created three concentric lakes around her hill. They got five pairs of twins, and he divided Atlantis in 10 parts.

The firstborn of the first pair, Atlas, got the central and best part, and became the supreme king. They named both the island and the ocean after him. The second of the first pair of twins got the outermost end of the island towards the pillars of Heracles, facing the land that is now called Gades in that part of the world. He got the name Gadeiros in their tongue—Eumelos in Greek—and Gades is named after him.

The next pair got the names Ampheres and Evaemon, the third pair Mneseus and Autochthon (which means native). The fourth pair was called Elasippus and Mestor, and the fifth Azaes and Diaprepes. All these and their heirs in many generations were inhabitants and rulers on various islands in the open ocean, but also inside the pillars as far as Egypt and Tyrrhenia.

The kingdom was passed on from Atlas to the oldest son for many generations. They possessed a wealth like no other potentate had before them, and probably nobody ever will again. Most was produced on the island, and other items were imported.

From the earth they dug out whatever was to be found there, solid as well as fusile, and that which is now only a name and was then something more than a name—orichalcum—was dug out of the earth in many parts of the island, being more precious in those days than anything except gold. There was an abundance of timber for the carpenters, and plenty of food for wild and tame animals. Even the largest of all animals, the elephant, thrived on the island. There were all kinds of

11

fruits and seeds in abundance, and pulse was cultivated.

They constructed temples, palaces, harbours, and docks. They built a palace for the god and their ancestors, which they continued to improve for successive generations, until the building had become a wonder to behold for its size and beauty. From the sea they dug a canal, 300 feet wide and 100 feet deep and 50 stadia long, to the first of the three concentric lakes (I have skipped a lot of details in this section, as I consider it highly unlikely that all of these measures actually reflect the situation on Atlantis; rather, it is probably an idealization on the part of Plato). The central island, on which the palace was located, had a diameter of five stadia. Each zone was surrounded by a stone wall, and the stone they quarried on location; some white, some black, and some red. The outermost wall they covered with brass, the middle with tin, and the third one flashed with the red light of orichalcum.[*]

As for the palaces, they will be of such vital importance in the following that I quote this literally:

The palaces in the interior of the citadel were constructed on this wise: In the centre was a holy temple dedicated to Cleito and Poseidon, which remained inaccessible and was surrounded by an enclosure of gold; this was the spot where the family of the ten princes first saw the light, and thither the people annually brought the fruits of the earth in their season from all the ten portions, to be an offering to each of the ten. Here was Poseidon's own temple which was a stadium in length, and half a stadium in width, and

---

[*] There is something odd here, since brass was not known until late in the Bronze Age, and simultaneously, *orichalkos* is the modern Greek word for brass. A later chapter is completely devoted to this topic.

of a proportionate height, having a strange, barbaric appearance. All the outside of the temple, with the exception of the pinnacles, they covered with silver, and the pinnacles with gold. In the interior of the temple the roof was of ivory, curiously wrought everywhere with gold and silver and orichalcum; and all the other parts, the walls and pillars and floor, they coated with orichalcum.

In the temple, they placed statues of gold. There was one of the god himself standing in a chariot—the charioteer of six winged horses—surrounded by one hundred Nereids riding on dolphins. There was also an altar, in corresponding size and splendour, and the palaces matched the glory of the temples and the size of the kingdom.

The next zone was used for baths, both open and covered, to be used as warm baths during the winter. In a similar way, Plato went on for several more paragraphs, before he went over to describing the rest of the island.

The whole island was high and steep on the side of the sea, but at and around the city the surrounding was a plain, which in turn was surrounded by mountains that sloped down to the sea. The hills on the island were gently rolling, and the island had an elongate shape, three thousand stadia long and two thousand across in the centre of the island. The part of the island with the plain was open to the South, but protected from the North. The surrounding mountains were famous for their number, size, and beauty, far beyond anything that still exists. In them, there were many prosperous villages, and brooks and lakes and meadows.

The kings had absolute power each in his dominion. The law was written down on a pillar of orichalcum at the temple of Poseidon. The kings gathered there every fifth and every sixth year alternately, to discuss common matters and to pass judgment. They would sacrifice a bull over the pillar with the law, and swear oaths. At nightfall, they dressed in azure robes and passed judgment in the darkness of the night. When the daybreak came, the verdicts were written down on a golden tablet.

The most important law was that they should not wage war against one another, and that they should all come to the rescue if any of their cities should try to overthrow the royal house.

After this, Plato went over to describing why they started the war against Athens, but he finished the book mid-paragraph. These are the last complete paragraphs:

They despised everything but virtue, caring little for their present state of life, and thinking lightly of the possession of gold and other property, which seemed only a burden to them; neither were they intoxicated by luxury; nor did wealth deprive them of their self-control; but they were sober, and saw clearly that all these goods are increased by virtue and friendship with one another, whereas by too great regard and respect for them, they are lost and friendship with them. [...] but when the divine portion began to fade away, and became diluted too often and too much with the mortal admixture, and the human nature got the upper hand, they then, being unable to bear their fortune, behaved unseemly, and to him who had an eye to see, grew visibly debased, for they were losing the fairest of their precious gifts; but to those who had no eye to see the true happiness, they appeared glorious and blessed at the very time when they were full of avarice and unrighteous power.

These are, in summary, the facts we have available to work with. Let us now see what can be done with this information. Remember that the scientific method requires us to try to prove that the hypothesis is wrong, not that it is right. Only if we fail in all tests, can we accept it as possibly being true.

Testing the Hypothesis

There are of course certain details in Plato's description that do not match Ireland, but are these discrepancies relevant as arguments for falsifying the hypothesis? No, because one has to allow Plato, Solon, and others to remember wrong and make certain mistakes, without presuming that everything else also is falsehood.

In other words, no argument against the hypothesis is valid, that is based on that some phenomena existed on Atlantis but not on Ireland. First, because it could be that our knowledge about ancient Ireland is inadequate. Second, because Plato could have received a contaminated myth. Third, it could be a detail invented by Plato—in fact, describing a utopia was the stated purpose of the dialog, and so everything that is "too good to be true" probably belongs to this category. A good example is "man-made canals 100 feet deep". I had the opportunity to board the world's largest dredgers when supervising the building of the bridge between Sweden and Denmark. Thirty metres dredging depth still is on the limit of science fiction.

It would also be an invalid argument if Plato has neglected to mention something that we know existed on Ireland. The only arguments that are both valid and relevant are those that compare details identified *both* on Atlantis and on Ireland, thereby allowing a quantitative comparison. Only that method allows us to calculate if the correspondence is significantly better than we would

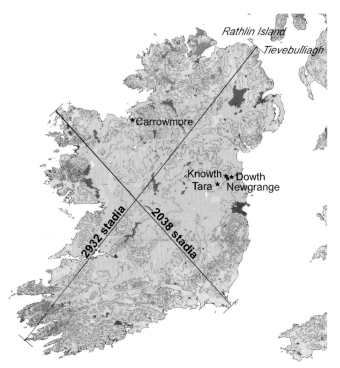

Ireland with the length and width marked in stadia (166 m). Since the coast is generally steep, the size has hardly been affected by post-glacial land uplift or sea-level rise. Contour interval 150 m.

expect from pure chance. The size of the island fulfils this criterion, why we start with that.

Island size and shape

Let us first look at the shape of Ireland. Atlantis should be elongated, and so is Ireland. The length of Atlantis was 3,000 stadia, and it was 2,000 stadia wide at the middle. How long is a stadium? It is 100 fathoms, or 200 yards, or 300 ell, or 600 feet. But whose feet? Since the hypothesis is that Atlantis was the empire of the megalith people, we should of course use *their* feet.

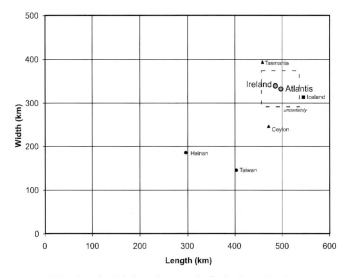

Maximal length and width for Atlantis, and all islands on this planet that are of a similar size, and compact shape. Tasmania and Ceylon are triangular and thus not widest over the middle. Iceland has a large peninsula in the northwest. The uncertainty, 250 stadia, is based on a precision of 1.5 digits.

By measuring the construction dimensions in a large number of megalith monuments, Alexander Thom in *Megalithic Sites in Britain* (1967) concluded that they used a yard of 0.829 m as the basic measuring unit. He coined the term megalithic yard for it. With time, the measure has slowly drifted away from its original value, so that a megalithic yard corresponds to about 2 ft 8 5/8 inch in modern-day Imperial units.

A megalithic stadium is thus about 166 m. As shown on the map, Ireland is 2,932 stadia long and 2,038 stadia wide at the middle. The difference is less than 3% compared to Atlantis—in both dimensions. It is obvious that the hypothesis survived this test (which it would even if we had used modern Imperial units), but out of

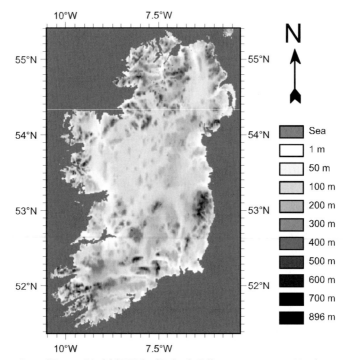

Digital Terrain Model (DTM) of Ireland. Cell size 0.5 minute in North-South, 1 minute in East-West (which makes the island look a bit compressed in the latter direction).

curiosity one might ask just how unlikely the correspondence is.

Islands of this size are not very common on Earth. Even less so if we only consider those of compact shape. By comparing the length and width of all suitable candidates (regardless of ocean) to that of Atlantis, it becomes obvious that the correspondence between Ireland and Atlantis is truly astonishing.

However, it was statistics we wanted: What is the probability that this correspondence could be caused by pure chance? For this calculation, we assume that (1)

Plato picked a length and width at random, with only one significant digit; (2) the width is always less than the length; (3) the length is between 700 and 10,000 stadia; and (4) the width is at least 600 stadia. We then get 91 possible values of the size of the island, equivalent to a probability of 1.1% that it was pure chance, against 98.9% that Plato really knew Ireland's dimensions. One can argue back and forth about how different assumptions would affect the value, but it remains obvious that the hypothesis passes the traditional 95% confidence level.

Landscape

Plato gave quite a few pieces of information regarding the landscape. Is there anything that can be used for hypothesis testing? Well, there is one peculiar feature: That the plain was in the centre of the island, surrounded by mountains that sloped down into the sea. Normally the situation is of course the reverse on islands: The mountains are in the centre.

Using a Digital Terrain Model (DTM), the morphology of Ireland was analyzed. After inspecting both the absolute elevation (to identify the mountains) and the slope angle (to identify the plain), the verdict was unequivocal: Ireland fits the description like hand in glove. There are many details that fit, such as the steep cliffs on the seaward coast (see the book's front cover), the gentler slopes on the other coasts, and that the central valley has a view to the sea while being surrounded by rolling mountains (there used to be villages in them during the Stone Age, before peat growth—induced by the agriculture—destroyed the fertility).

Once more, what is the statistical probability that Plato was right by chance? Let us pick just one aspect, one that is easy to quantify and identify: That the plain was in the centre surrounded by mountains. On a DTM with 2-minute resolution, a search was made for islands that are lower in the inland than by the coast. Analysing the 50 largest islands on this planet, exactly one fulfilled the criteria: Ireland. Statistically, this means that the probability was only 2% that Ireland would match this characteristic by chance.

Result

If we combine the results so far, the joint probability that the match is due to chance is only one in 4641. Stated in another way, the probability is over 99.98% that the island of Atlantis is identical to Ireland. This is based only on its length, its width, and the fact that a central plain is surrounded by mountains.

Other details that match are the rolling mountains (only some combinations of geological history and climate produce rolling mountains), and that both Atlantis and Ireland are widest over the middle. If we were to calculate in the same way for these and other factors, there is probably a bigger risk of being struck by the lightening, than that Atlantis matches Ireland by pure chance. Speaking of which, it is often said that the risk of being struck by lightening is one in a million. Actually, that is not quite accurate. The risk is three in a million (as part of a natural-disaster mitigation project in Nicaragua, in which we tried to quantify all natural hazards, I calculated that 3 persons die for each million lightenings in the U.S.).

If you stayed alert, you will have noted that it is only the first line of the hypothesis that has been tested: That the island Atlantis was Ireland. The second part, that the

Atlantic Empire is associated with the megalith culture, has not yet been tested. The argument of the sceptics could be that Plato knew about Ireland from a later source, and made the empire up. As you will see in the following chapters, there are many things that speak against such an interpretation, but there is one argument in particular which unequivocally supports the hypothesis, and against which I have not been able to formulate any counter-argument: The fact that Atlantis sank in the sea.

The Sunken Island

For many people, the most conspicuous characteristic of Atlantis is that the island sank in the sea. Actually, it is not such a big deal. The world sea level rose by at least 60 m when the Ice Age ended, so many islands must have sunk in the sea at that time. The task here is just to find out which one is hiding behind the Atlantis myth. It is obviously not Ireland, because last time I flew over it, it was still distinctly above the sea surface.

Let me tell you a story about another place, the North Sea. The southern half of the North Sea is shallow, and during the Ice Age, it was dry land. That is, Scotland was a peninsula on the European continent. Woolly mammoth, woolly rhinoceros, European bison, reindeer, and lions lived on what is now the bottom of the sea. And man.

As the Ice Age ended, the sea level started rising. Great Britain was cut off from the continent. A long peninsula extended from the base of Jutland and northern Germany, almost to England. As the sea kept rising, the end of the peninsula became an island, about 250 km long and 100 km wide. This island existed well into

21

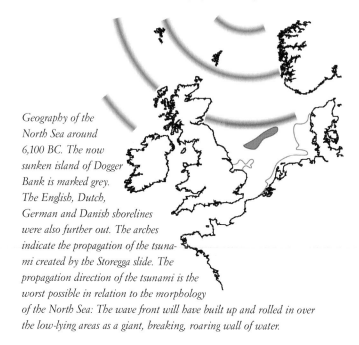

Geography of the North Sea around 6,100 BC. The now sunken island of Dogger Bank is marked grey. The English, Dutch, German and Danish shorelines were also further out. The arches indicate the propagation of the tsunami created by the Storegga slide. The propagation direction of the tsunami is the worst possible in relation to the morphology of the North Sea: The wave front will have built up and rolled in over the low-lying areas as a giant, breaking, roaring wall of water.

postglacial times, during the early climatic optimum.

Life was good during this time. Flint tool production in southern Scandinavia—where some of the best flint in Europe is found—reached its zenith. Only big game was hunted, indicating an easy life with lots of leisure time. The summers were warm and hot, the climate much better than the present. Perhaps by coincidence, geologists call this the Atlantic Time. But, say the joy that lasts forever.

Around 6,100 BC, a giant sub-marine landslide known as the Storegga slide occurred off Norway. It set off a tsunami, long-period ocean waves as indicated on the map. When such waves reach a gradually rising sea bottom, they grow in height into destructive walls of water. The bottom of the North Sea is gently sloping to the north, meaning that the tsunami was maximally reinforced.

Just after this took place in the North Sea, living conditions in southern Scandinavia deteriorated significantly. The population density grew, the flint tools started to be mass-produced without the same care for quality, and they started to hunt also small game. They even ate fish; before they had only hunted larger sea animals. It is hard not to suspect a correlation with the event in the North Sea: An exodus of survivors from a devastating natural disaster, the likeness of which we have not seen in Europe in historic times. The area around the North Sea is today the most densely populated in Europe. There is no reason to suspect that it was not the case already at that time.

In addition, the northern islands of Orkney have since sunk due to sea-level rise. Back then, the cliffs that now form an archipelago, were mountains on a low-lying plain. That area, too, was struck hard by the tsunami.

However dramatic the tsunami may have been, the water must have withdrawn after some hours. A tsunami cannot make an island sink. Alas, it was not the only dramatic and exceptional event of the time.

As the inland ice in North America melted away, a melt-water lake was formed over Canada, Lake Agassiz. The remaining ice in Hudson Bay prevented it from flowing out into the ocean. Until one day, around 6,100 BC, the lake was discharged. So large was the lake, that the world sea level rose by about one foot just from the water. If the outburst pulled with it large amounts of ice, which it likely did, the sea level may have risen even more.

Did these two events take place at the same time? Maybe. Perhaps a chain of events triggered one from the other, or both from a third event, such as an earthquake or a meteorite shower. Finds of micro spherules in peat on the Estonian island of Hiiumaa (Swedish: Dagö) have been dated to this same time, within some centuries. They are minute glass pearls that may form when meteorites explode in the atmosphere. Thus, a "heavenly" origin of the event is conceivable. Meteorites could have set off earthquakes in both Europe and Canada within minutes from each other.

What we know for a fact is that the island sank in the sea, that a tsunami hit the area, and that these two events occurred within some centuries from each other, that is, within the precision of the dating method. Plato did claim that Atlantis had sunk in an earthquake, so that an impassable mud bank remained, preventing the passage "from here" to any part of the ocean.

A tsunami of the magnitude observed in the geological record will have pulled out enormous amounts of debris to the sea. The recently sunken island will have remained as a mud bank. Thus, Plato's claim that the sea was un-navigable is reasonable. Since Dogger Bank is not in front of the Straits of Gibraltar, perhaps we should consider more seriously the claim that the pillars of Heracles are located in northwestern Europe, somewhere near the German North Sea shore. Is it Helgoland, perhaps?

The time gap between the sinking of the island, and the oldest known megalith tomb on Ireland, is less than 500 years. Megaliths of about the same age are found in westernmost France and the Iberian Peninsula.

Conclusion

Apparently, the myth of a sunken island is not a myth

about Atlantis, but a myth *from* Atlantis. The tale is contaminated with earlier elements.

This suggests that also some of the other details could refer to Dogger Bank rather than to Ireland. The first thing that comes to mind is the presence of elephants. There are no elephants on Ireland, but mammoth tusks have been found on Dogger Bank. If also this element of the myth is *from* Atlantis, then perhaps we should look for traditions of a sunken island in Irish folklore.

Plato wrote that Poseidon created three concentric lakes around a central hill with his trident. Now, Poseidon was of course originally also the "earth-shaker", the god of earthquakes. Earthquakes result when meteorites hit land or water, and the trident is apparently the metaphor of a meteorite (in later myth perhaps replaced by Zeus' thunderbolt).

When a meteorite hits land, a crater is formed. When it hits water, waves are formed. Logically, if it hits plastic water-laden sediments of the right viscosity, waves start forming but become "frozen", so that three concentric lakes are formed. The centre swings up and down, and if it runs out of energy at the right moment, a hill will form. It appears theoretically possible. That is, it is only possible on the bottom of the North Sea, where there is plenty of soft sediments. On Ireland, I do not think it would have been possible. Thus, this too must be expected to be a detail from the sunken island, if it has any background in reality.

According to Irish mythology, the Partholanians were the first race of man to live on Ireland. They conquered the island from the Fomorians, giants and pirates. Partholan, son of Sera, is said to have arrived to Ireland from the western land of the living beyond the sea, where men continue their existence after death. He came with his queen Dealgnaid. The myth says that Ireland *physically was another land* at that time than it is now. There were but *three lakes*, nine rivers, and one single plain.

Amazingly, it seems possible that the memory of the sunken island has survived also on Ireland, although in a different form, hazier from the passing of time. If this myth, that would pre-date the megalith culture according to this interpretation, has survived *both* on Ireland and in Plato's dialogs, then he cannot reasonably have invented the Atlantic Empire. Furthermore, the fact that Plato appears to have had more accurate information than the Irish, strongly suggests that the memory has been preserved elsewhere, in written form—and why not at the temple in Sais?

Just a little clarification: This does not mean that the Partholanians used to live on Dogger Bank. I would rather guess that they are quite recent immigrants, perhaps as late as the Bronze Age. It is probably just a typical case of mixing mythological elements from different times.

Recently, an hypothesis for the location of Atlantis in the Straits of Gibraltar has been advanced by Collina-Girard (2001). The Spartel Island, 14 x 5 km, sank in the rising sea slightly before 9,000 BC. It was located in the mouth of a longer Straits of Gibraltar, which they argue agrees well with Plato's tale.

It is curious that two sunken islands both are located off the Columns of Heracles. One might speculate if perhaps the memory of Spartel Island was transposed to the North Sea some time in the dawn of pre-history, and the name of Heracles with it. Nevertheless, a later transposition for another reason is vastly more probable.

Regarding the time, most students assume that Atlantis went under 9,000 years before Solon's visit to Sais, since Plato wrote that in Critias. However, Plato contradicted himself. In Timeaus, he wrote that Athens was founded 9,000 years before, and Sais 8,000 years before. Furthermore, Atlantis attacked both Athens and Sais (and Athens defeated Atlantis).

Disregarding the unlikelihood that Athens would win a war against the world's greatest super-power on the year of its own foundation, it is outright improbable that someone would attack Sais 1,000 years before that city was founded.

Collina-Girard's argument is based on that the time was right, but the measurement units were mistaken. However, Atlantis' proportions were 2:3, while Spartel Island was closer to 1:3. That difference can hardly be caused by a mistake in measurement units.

Some elements of the Atlantis tale might reflect the Spartel event, even though it happened pretty long time ago. Nevertheless, from what has been presented here it is obvious that the majority of quantifiable details do not match.

Lost Continents

While on the subject of the sunken island, let me just briefly mention that there is no such thing as a sunken continent. After the advent of deep sea research (pioneered by the Swedish *Albatross* expedition in 1947 – 1948) there is no longer any room for hesitation. We now know how ocean bottoms are formed through plate tectonics, and we know the morphology of the oceans in significant detail. There is simply no room for any *sunken* continent in the oceans.

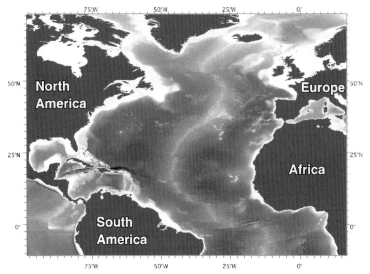

A DTM (digital terrain model) of the ocean floor in the North Atlantic. The grey scale is linear, and black is only used for the largest depths (north of Puerto Rico). The continental shelf is near white; it was exposed (dry land) during the Ice Age. Note the Mid-Atlantic Ridge (which Iceland is part of).

A *lost* continent, though, is quite another cup of tea. If early Europeans knew about America, and the contacts were discontinued for one reason or another, then America will have been lost for Europeans, and Europe will have been lost for Americans.

Thus, even if there were myths on both sides of the Atlantic speaking of a lost continent in that ocean, there would still not be any logical reason to infer that an entire continent had disappeared. The simplest explanation would instead be that early *trans-Atlantic seafaring* had come to an end.

2. Poseidon's Temples

If Atlantis was megalithic Ireland, then what Plato wrote should match what we find in Ireland, at least to some extent. If it is incompatible, then we should reject the second part of the hypothesis, the part regarding the time of Atlantis.

So let us try to link the architecture of Atlantis to the archaeology of Ireland. For the first time since Plato's time, tourists can now look at the "marvels" that he described. Let me just disappoint you about one detail: Somebody beat us to the gold. We must not expect to find any of the precious metals of Atlantis.

Central Ireland features a roughly rectangular lowland, delimited by Galway in the southwest, Dublin in the southeast, Dundalk in the northeast, and Ballina in the northwest. On the eastern part of the plain there is a hill called Tara. It is about 150 m high, and not very conspicuous. On its top, there is a megalithic tomb, some circular ditches, and a pillar that is known as the Stone of Destiny. According to Irish mythology, Tara was the seat of the kings in the olden days.

Plato wrote that the king came from a low mountain with gentle slopes. Sounds like it could be Tara, does it not? Furthermore, he mentioned a temple for

Central Ireland. Contour interval 500 feet (ca 150 m).

Poseidon and the ancestors, on a place that is open to the south but protected from the north. Well, one hundred stadia from Tara we find the finest megalithic monuments anywhere: Newgrange, Knowth and Dowth. Those are passage tombs located on the northern side of the river Boyne, that is, on a south slope. It is understood that a tomb that you can walk into is in fact a temple for the ancestors, with another terminology.

The oldest megalithic monuments on Ireland are, however, located in the northwest, near present-day Sligo. Archaeological excavations in the last decades have given some ^{14}C (radioactive-carbon dating) ages from the sixth millennium BC. There are successively younger concentrations of megalithic tombs on the central plain of Ireland, in a traverse from the northwest to the south-

© Martin Byrne

In this region, farthest out on Cúil Irra, beyond Carrowmore, lays the mountain Knocknarea. On its flat top, 327 m (1,073 ft) above the sea, sits Miosgan Meadhbha, 'Queen Maeve's Cairn', a megalithic tomb that—challenged only by Newgrange—is the most magnificent on Ireland, with its diameter of 60 m (200 ft), and high profile. The shape with a flat top is presumably original. It has never been excavated.

east and Boyne. Megalithic tombs are spread out all over Ireland, but when looking for the ancient capital of Atlantis, only Sligo can even begin to compete with the Boyne valley in Co. Meath. So let us start in Co. Sligo, giving precedence to age (Co. means county).

Miosgan Meadhbha

'Queen Maeve's Cairn' sits on the top of the prominent mountain Knocknarea in North Sligo, at the seaward end of the peninsula Cúil Irra. In the middle of the peninsula, there is a field of dolmens and stone circles. Only 27 remain today, but at least 65 are known.

The Carrowmore field has been excavated by Swedish archaeologists, who have obtained ^{14}C-dates between 5,400 and 3,500 BC (Bergh, 1995). That would make this one of the oldest megalith areas in Europe. Irish archaeologists have expressed doubts about the older of these dates, but later a still older ^{14}C-date has been obtained from a cairn on the top of the mountain Croughaun (or Croghaun): 5,650 BC.

Queen Maeve's Cairn is said to be named after a ferocious Iron Age Queen, supposedly buried there. The most prominent monument in this region, it is believed to be built around 4,000 BC.

Dolmen at Carrowmore.

© Kathleen Laraia McLaughlin, 1999

The fact that it has not been plundered—at least not since the Iron Age—is thought to be a result of the respect that Queen Maeve had. Of course, the claim that an Iron Age queen is buried in a Stone Age tomb raises a warning flag. This could be a mix-up of two myths: That about a dreaded grave where the ancestral mother was buried, and that about the dreaded queen. The two ideas resembled each other too much, and were merged. That is what I think. Only an archaeological excavation can clarify what is really hiding under the stones.

It is characteristic that the monuments are often on the very summit of the mountains. It is perhaps not so odd, if one considers that a tsunami hit the area less than 500 years before the first ones were built. Furthermore, the sea level rose much faster on southern Ireland than northern. Perhaps the ancients were aware of this. One can speculate that it contributed to them placing the monuments high, and in the north rather than in the south.

Having visited the oldest monuments, we will now turn our attention to the finest on the island.

Boyne Valley

Within an 8 km² (3 sq.mi.) large area in Co. Meath, there are over 30 pre-historic monuments, including

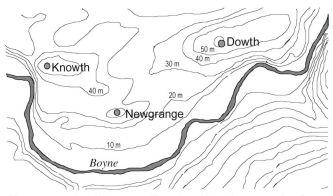

The passage tombs of Newgrange, Knowth and Dowth are located on low hills to the north of the river Boyne. There are also about 18 satellite tombs around Knowth, standing stones, etc.

three large so-called passage tombs. This is an area of good soil for agriculture, unlike Sligo, where the marine food gathering was dominating. The change in place coincides with the shift to agriculture as the main source of subsistence, that is, the shift from what archaeologists call a Mesolithic to a Neolithic society.

Dowth is assumed the oldest, followed by Knowth, which is the largest. Newgrange is the most spectacular, though. The construction in the valley may have started as early as 3,800 BC. These monuments represent the climax of the megalith tradition, for sure in Ireland, and probably in all of Europe.

Around 2,800 BC, just when the megalith culture vanished, there was a marked climatic decline, including in northwestern Europe. Archaeologists suspect this to be the direct cause of the cultural change, and of the demise of the megalith culture.

The architecture of the Boyne Valley passage tombs is similar to that of the megalithic passage tombs of the

View from the top of Dowth to Newgrange. The Irish name is "Brú na Bóinne", 'the Mansion of Boyne' (other possible translations include 'the Palace' and 'the Hostel').

northern European Funnel Beaker Culture. Standing giant stones form a passage and a chamber, and giant stone slabs form a roof. However, there are also differences. Whereas Scandinavian passage tombs can have rectangular chambers covered by several enormous granite blocks, sometimes 6 m long and 1 m think, the largest passage tombs on Ireland have cross-shaped chambers covered by a corbelled vault (a "false vault" created by overlapping stones). This feature they have in common with the so-called tholos tombs, of the Mycenaean (Late Bronze Age) culture in Greece. However, the Irish ones are of course almost 2,000 years older.

To learn more about the landscape with the pre-historic heritage and the ancient monuments along the Boyne river, I suggest Stout (2003), *Newgrange and the bend of the Boyne.*

Newgrange. The white is quartz, most of it added as part of the restoration.

Brú na Bóinne

Newgrange is the most spectacular, best known, first discovered, last built, and most visited, why it will be given precedence. It is even one of the finest passage graves in all of Europe. Although already here my pen may have slipped, since it has been suggested that it is not a grave after all. For instance, O'Brien (1834, p. 351) considered it a temple for a mystery cult, and O'Callaghan (2004) argued that it was a "temple to life". This reflects the dominating opinion today according to an on-line inquiry in Ireland, in spite of scholars through centuries calling it a tomb. Amateurs insist that it is no more a grave, than is a Christian cathedral that contains burials.

It has also been called the oldest still standing building in the world, meaning continuously having had a roof. It was built around 3,100 BC, half a millennium before the pyramids of Egypt. It was already older in Plato's days, than Parthenon in Athens is today.

The entrance to Newgrange, with the carved stone and the light opening over the door. There were flat stone slabs for closing both the door opening (visible to the right of the door) and the rectangular window.

© Celestial Panoramas Ltd / Alamy

Newgrange has a diameter of 85 m, and is 13,5 m high. It is located on the top of a low hill. Around the base, there are 97 large boulders or kerbstones, some of which are engraved with geometrical patterns. The most prominent engraving is on the stone in front of the entrance.

The entrance is oriented towards the point on the horizon where the sun rises at winter solstice. The rectangular window over the door opening allows the sun to enter the inner chamber during 2-3 weeks around winter solstice. Since the 19 m long passage is sloping up, the light from the door itself does not reach that far. Many want to see the midwinter sunrise inside the chamber, but few can, since the space inside is limited.

Detail of the stone in front of the entrance to Newgrange.

The chamber is shaped like a cross, 6.5 x 6.2 m. Remains of two burials were found in its centre. The stone basins in the chamber recesses have been used for ritual purposes.

For further reading I would suggest Uistin (2000), *Exploring Newgrange,* for the one who just wants to flesh this description out a bit. For those seriously interested in going to the core of the mound so to say, O'Kelly (1995), *Newgrange: Archaeology, Art and Legend,* is written by the archaeologist who did most of the excavations.

Comparison with Atlantis

Poseidon's temple was one stadium long and a half wide, according to Plato, was located on a hill, and had "a strange, barbaric appearance". Can this be reconciled?

Newgrange is round with a diameter of 0.51 stadium (85 m), which is as close to the correct width as one can possibly expect to get. As to the "strange, barbaric appearance", that is of course a matter of taste; but if

37

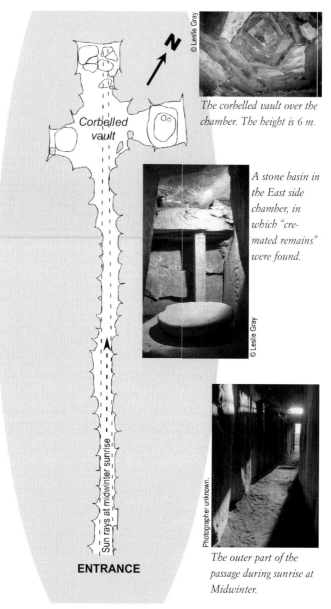

© Leslie Gray

The corbelled vault over the chamber. The height is 6 m.

A stone basin in the East side chamber, in which "cremated remains" were found.

© Leslie Gray

Sun rays at midwinter sunrise

ENTRANCE

Photographer unknown.

The outer part of the passage during sunrise at Midwinter.

Plan of the passage of Newgrange.

Parthenon was the model for a temple, I suppose everyone would call Newgrange "strange". The hill also matches, but the one thing that does not match is the length. Allow me to speculate why.

During classical times, buildings were rectangular. In the megalith period, they were all round—incidentally, this also applied to Mycenaean tholos tombs with their false vaults. If you would give the size of Newgrange, what would you say (without using the loan word diameter)? Perhaps you would say that it was "half a stadium across". If the listener assumed that all temples were rectangular, how would he interpret this? Presumably that you referred to the width. Plato would thus have had to invent a length to fit the width. Does it make sense?

My conclusion, at least, is that Newgrange very well may have been Poseidon's temple.

Speaking of him, those who wrote in Linear B (in Mycenae, Knossos, and other Late Bronze Age palaces in Greece) used the name Poseidon, and so did Homer. Homer once mentioned (Iliad 1:403) the hundred-handed giant whom the gods call Briareus, but whom all men call Aegaeon (Gr. Aigaìon). It has been suggested that he was Poseidon's son; others say it was his nickname. The Aegean Sea is of course named after him, as is the island of Aegina. The name resembles the Nordic name of the sea god, Aegir (Ægir, Ägir).

The Irish equivalent is apparently Manannan mac Lir, god of the sea and fertility, who forecasts the weather. He is the son of Lir and his name means 'Manannan Son of the Sea'. His wife is Fand and he is the foster-father of many gods, including Lugh. He is the guardian of the Blessed Isles, and the ruler of Mag Mell.

39

© Holy McGrail

A satellite in the foreground to the left, and the main mound at Knowth.

Manannan has a ship that follows his command without sails; his cloak makes him invisible; his helmet is made of flames and his sword cannot be turned from its mark. He is described as riding over the sea in a chariot, which fits with Plato's words that there was a statue of Poseidon as charioteer in his temple, surrounded by a hundred Nereids (incidentally, the Greeks only believed there to be fifty Nereids).

Amazingly, Newgrange is known as the *mansion* locally, while Plato wrote about a *palace*. Is it an over 5,000 year old tradition, or is it a coincidence?

Knowth

Knowth is the largest passage tomb, not just in the Boyne Valley but also in all of Ireland. The central mound is 95 m in north south, and 85 m in east west (0.57 and 0.51 stadium, respectively).

Around the base, there are 127 kerb stones, including directly in front of the entrances to the passages. The mound has two passages and two chambers, one from the east and one from the west. Both the passages are longer than any other on Ireland is. The mound was excavated starting in 1960, and was opened again for visitors in May of 2003.

The eastern passage was built narrow, but became even narrower when some of the standing boulders started to slant inwards. They can now only be passed by crawling on the ground. The passage leads to a cross-

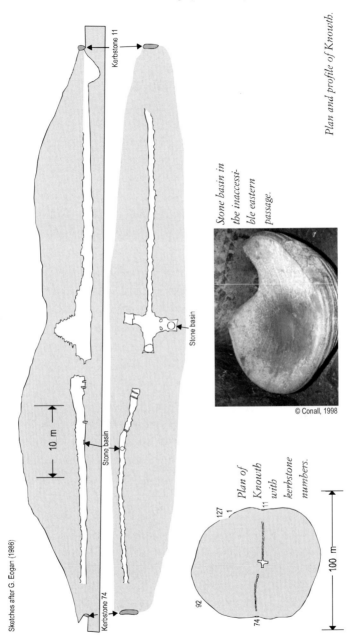

Plan and profile of Knowth.

Stone basin in the inaccessible eastern passage.

© Conall, 1998

Kerbstone 11

Stone basin

10 m

Stone basin

Sketches after G. Eogan (1986)

Kerbstone 74

Plan of Knowth with kerbstone numbers.

127
1
11
92
74

100 m

41

shaped chamber with a corbelled vault.

In one of the alcoves of the chamber, there is a round, concave stone basin with traces of fire. The archaeologists, who traditionally have regarded Knowth as a tomb, have guessed that this stone has been used for cremations.

Knowth is filled with rock carvings, both inside the passages, on the surrounding kerbstones, and on the 17 – 19 satellite mounds (there are different opinions about their number). The motives are spirals, zigzag lines etc. It is the richest site on Ireland when it comes to rock carvings. About half of all carvings on the island have been found at this one site.

It has been suggested, that Knowth may have served as a library for Stone Age knowledge, and that some symbols are identical to symbols found as far away as in tropical Africa and among the aborigines in Australia.

This is of course no proof of contact; it is quite possible that they have portrayed the same real-life feature, a portent that may have been visible everywhere. At Järrestad, in the megalith area of southern Scandinavia, similar spirals and zigzag lines have been found. The one on the front cover of the book is from there. In my opinion, it depicts a spinning comet visible from the entire planet. It is positioned in the way that it might have appeared once upon a time, shortly before dawn.

There are almost one hundred burials in Knowth. The many satellites suggest that the place may have been used over a long period. In fact, the archaeologists have concluded that one satellite has been rebuilt in order to make place for the main mound the way it is today. This means that at least some of the satellites are older than at least a part of the main mound. That might potentially be important for the interpretation.

On the floor of the eastern passage in the central mound, there is a large stone that may have had an astronomical significance. It presumably was put in place long before the mound was built.

Archaeologists typically give age estimates with the uncertainty of the dating method (for instance 3,100 ± 150 BC). However, large projects such as this may well have taken longer time to build than the uncertainty in the ^{14}C dating method. Building at Knowth started no later than 3,800 BC, and stopped no earlier than 3,100 BC.

To learn more about Knowth, I suggest Eogan (1987), *Knowth and passage-tombs of Ireland*, written by the excavator of the mounds.

Comparison with Atlantis

If Newgrange could be Poseidon's temple, or perhaps his palace (or both), Knowth could rather be the temple of the ancestral earth-born mother and divine father: Cleito and Poseidon. The central mound logically might be for them and perhaps for the closest relatives, while the satellites might be for lesser dignitaries.

As you may recall, Plato wrote that each king improved and beautified the temple. This matches what we know about Knowth.

Furthermore, Plato wrote, "In the centre was a holy temple dedicated to Cleito and Poseidon, which remained inaccessible..." As we have seen, the eastern passage of Knowth is inaccessible. From a geotechnical point of view, one may assume that the movement of the stone slabs occurred rather early after the construction of the passage tomb, already in Neolithic times. Thus, it is quite possible that Plato got words about it. Incidentally,

Aerial view of Dowth. It is called Dubad in Gaelic, which means 'darkness'.

perhaps Newgrange was built precisely to replace the destroyed temple.

As for the two passages, one may speculate that the western one was the *home* (tomb) for the earth-born ancestral mother Cleito, while the eastern passage with its cross-shaped chamber and false vault was a *temple* for the immortal ancestral father, Poseidon. That would explain the similarity between the eastern passage in Knowth, and the presumably only passage in Newgrange.

Dowth

One last great passage tomb remains to be described: Dowth. The mound contains two passages, as was established during an un-professional excavation in 1847, which severely damaged the mound. Some work has also been done in the 1930s, but in modern time, no excavation has been carried out. There are plans, though, and the land was purchased in 1998 for that purpose.

Just as Knowth, Dowth was surrounded by a line of

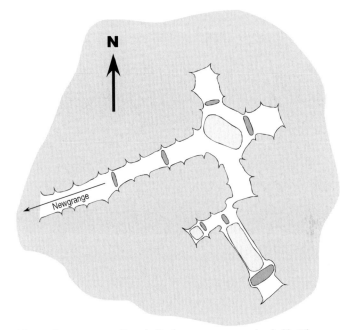

The northern passage in Dowth. Darker grey stones are thresholds. The entrance is to the left (now under ground).

kerbstones around its base, about 100 of them. The dimensions of Dowth are similar to those of Newgrange, 85 m in diameter and 15 m high.

Dowth thus has two passages, one northerly, and one southerly. The latter has a simple geometry with a passage leading to a chamber, and an opening that allows the sun to enter in mid afternoon during the winter. The chamber originally had a corbelled vault (like Newgrange and the eastern passage of Knowth), but it is now replaced by concrete. Outside the southern passage, the threshold stone is slanted, but a carved spiral still remains visible.

The opening of the northern passage is at present under the ground outside the mound. The passage is the

© Michael Fox, 2001

Inside the more southerly of the two passages in Dowth. The roof is not original.

most complicated on Ireland, and quite possibly of all megalithic tombs in Europe. The main passage leads to a cross-shaped chamber, but in the right arm of it, there is a small opening to yet another narrow passage, leading to a second chamber. The main passage is aligned to the sunset during midwinter solstice, but also to Newgrange.

Comparison with Atlantis

Dowth is considered the oldest one of the three, and resembles Knowth in having two passages, and a corbelled vault in the easterly one. If Knowth was a temple for both the mortal and the immortal ancestor, Dowth may have had the same function.

So why a new mound? Perhaps Knowth represents a new dynasty. In that case, Dowth ought to have been discontinued more or less when Knowth started to be used. It will be interesting to see what the excavations may give as result.

Plato only mentioned two temples, and they fit better with Knowth and Newgrange than with Dowth. Perhaps this means that Dowth no longer was in use when the tale originated.

Some suspect that Newgrange, too, has a second passage on the western side, still to be discovered. However, if Plato's account—in my interpretation—is correct, and it really refers to Knowth and Newgrange, then there should be no western passage of Newgrange. It should primarily be a temple or a palace, not a tomb. The two burials found there might represent some unique persons that were considered semi-divine—kind of like the Greek heroes.

To sum up, there is much that suggests that the Atlantic Empire indeed was associated with the megalithic culture, and that the capital was in Co. Meath, in the Boyne Valley, on Ireland—once the largest island in the Atlantic Ocean off Europe (that is, in those early days when England was still a part of the continent, and Scotland was a peninsula). Thus, the hypothesis survived the test. We cannot rule out that Atlantis was megalithic Ireland.

Consequently, the map on page 19 of the distribution of the megaliths, possibly represents the extension of the Atlantic Empire. From Sweden in the North, to Tunisia in the South; from Ireland in the West, to Malta in the East. Although Malta is just a dot on that map, it does have some of the most impressive megalith temples. However, this book ends where Plato ended, and therefore I will wait with those until the next book: The story that Plato did not tell us. The story of the war that Atlantis waged on the eastern Mediterranean. Because just as the Crusaders did much later, it is logical that the expedition started from the island of Malta.

A Swedish encyclopaedia defined Atlantis as a "fairy-tale land". The author had no idea how right he was—but not for the reason he thought. Ireland is the land of the fairy legends, and the megalithic mounds are the homes of the fairies in Irish legend. Thus, according to the hypothesis of this book, Atlantis really was the fairytale land—once upon a time.

If you excuse a bit of kitchen philosophy, consider how the phrase "Atlantis is a fairytale land" is true, even though—or rather, exactly because—Atlantis was real. What we have here could illustrate "newspeak," as coined by George Orwell in his *1984*. When the meaning of related words drift simultaneously, the texts remain true, and the change in meaning may not be detected.

If you have not guessed already, this is the pun of the book's subtitle. The fairy land that this book maps is very much of this world: The megalith culture of Ireland.

3. The King's Hill

In Plato's Atlantis, several functions were united in one place, centred on the hill of the earth-born man Evenor. However, we must bear in mind that elements from different times and places often are mixed up in legends. Thus, rather than finding one single place that matches perfectly, we might find various elements in different places. While Boyne seems to be the religious centre, there does not seem to be any seat of the king. Irish myth associates that with Tara, so let us turn our attention there.

Tara

One hundred stadia from the Boyne Valley we find Tara, the hill of the kings, with the legendary Stone of Destiny. This was the home of the kings in ancient times, according to Irish legends. Let us see what features from this place might appear in Plato's description of Atlantis.

Tara is an Anglo-Saxon form of Temair, and in Medieval texts the hill is alternately called Temair na ríg ('the King's Tara') and Temair Breg (after the plain Brega on which the hill is situated). The word "temair" can originally have meant 'point with a view' or 'holy place'. The hill is not very high, about 150 m and quite gentle, but it has a wide view over the Boyne Valley.

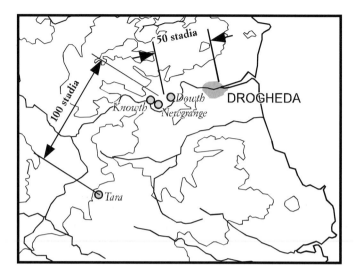

Tara is 100 stadia from the Boyne Valley passage tombs, and those are 50 stadia from the sea. The latter distance was mentioned by Plato.

Tara was the seat for the Irish supreme kings according to mythology—a mythology that was not written down until during the past millennium, though. According to the myth, the last people to conquer the island were the Milesians, who claimed to have met Moses in Egypt, and to have defeated the previous inhabitants, the Thuata de Danaan (or Danann). The latter people then made themselves invisible and became the fairies, living on in mounds and cairns.

According to a recently finished project, whose report *Tara: An Archaeological Survey* is due any time now, Tara was mainly used for rituals, and during four thousand years: From the Neolithic to early Christian times. Among the oldest remains is the cairn called Duma na nGiall ('Mound of the Hostages'). It reportedly has its name from a "tradition"(!) to exchange hostages there.

© Michael Fox, 2004

Aerial view of Tara. To the left in the larger circle is the Mound of the Hostages, in the centre the Inaugeration Hill with the Stone of Destiny. Taken in February, mid afternoon.

Inside the cairn, there are Neolithic rock carvings, including motifs of concentric circles. Archaeologists have guessed that it was built between 3,000 and 2,500 BC. They also guess that a circular palisade was built up to a thousand years earlier, but had burnt down before the cairn was built. A circle of holes from wooden poles indicates where the palisade used to be.

At Tara there is a famous pillar-like stone called Lia Fáil, 'Stone of Destiny'. Since 1824, it is standing in the centre of "Forrad", the 'Inauguration Hill,' but originally it is believed to have stood directly outside the entrance of the cairn, in the same way as one stone outside each of the two passages in Knowth.

Perhaps the idea was that the stones were to throw a

Entrance of the cairn at Tara, called Duma na nGiall, which means 'Mound of the Hostages'.

shadow into the cairn when the sun rose at the right place. Was it maybe a phallic symbol, symbolizing how the heavenly father fertilized the womb of Mother Earth?

Outside the entrance of the cairn, pots with the cremated remains of a number of persons were buried, before the passage was built. The chamber itself is 4 times 1 m, and subdivided into three compartments by low stones (this can be seen in many cairns). Each compartment contains the cremated remains of deceased, and gifts for the dead.

From this time, there is also a "cursus", a 'procession road,' called Tech Midchúarta. It is in line with the cairn.

Outside the area covered by the aerial view above, there is an enclosure consisting of a ditch with a bank on the outside, with a diameter of "almost 1000 m" (as a comparison, 6 stadia equals ca 996 m). This enclosure is known as Ráith na Ríg. The ditch is V-shaped and up to

Lia Fáil, the 'Stone of Destiny', at Tara. A phallic symbol, it has been suggested.

3.5 m deep. Leftover products from iron production have been found in the original bank fill, leading some to conclude that the enclosure was built after the introduction of iron. Frankly speaking, that is not a conclusion, that is a tautology; neither can it be wrong, nor does it add anything. So the question remains, when? Unfortunately, there does not seem to exist any ^{14}C or other independent dating.

The oral tradition on Ireland associates Tara with sacral kingship, and with the supreme king on Ireland, as in the first among equals, not as in the ruler of the others. It is expressed in the following way on the web site of The Discovery Programme: *A successful king of Tara, whose reign mirrored that of the universal ideal king, ruled justly, truthfully and prosperously.*

Comparison with Atlantis

The myth of Tara seems to have some things in common with the myth of Atlantis. Plato's whole idea with the

Atlantis dialogues was to describe an ideal order of things, and the myth about Tara is precisely that of an ideal monarchy, ruled by a king who was righteous and fair and who followed the law.

In Plato's Atlantis, there were ten kings, and one of them, the successor of Atlas, was the supreme king—not as a ruler over the others, but as the first among equals. There were several kings on Ireland, and the one in Tara had the same position relative his peers, as Atlas did on Atlantis. Note that not all of Atlantis' ten kings necessarily ruled on Atlantis itself; that number presumably included those who had their kingship overseas.

In Plato's Atlantis there was in the very centre a hill surrounded by a wall, 5 stadia in diameter, and a circular lake. In Tara there is a hill in the centre, once surrounded by a wall, later surrounded by a ditch and a bank, 6 stadia in diameter. In both places there were several concentric rings of earthwork.

In Plato's Atlantis there was a pillar of orichalcum (on which the law was inscribed) at Poseidon's temple in the centre of the island. In Tara there is a pillar-shaped stone, associated with the kingship, which probably stood by the cairn. The surface of it is so weathered, though, that if anything was written on it 5,000 years ago, it would presumably be long since gone.

The impression is that Tara resembles the hill where Evenor and Leucippe had their daughter Cleito. Allowing that details may be confused and mixed up, that the architecture may have slightly changed after the time when Plato's source was fixed so to say, and that parts of Plato's myth may refer to an earlier place and myth upon which also Tara was modelled, the conclusion is that the two places definitely are cognate, if not exactly the same.

What does this prove? It proves nothing, scientifically speaking. However, it strongly suggests that the mythology of Atlantis was based on a real place with its very real mythology. It was not made up. Thus, there is a high likelyhood that Atlantis existed in Neolithic Ireland, with the empire stretching all over megalithic Europe. Tara and Boyne were the centre, each playing a different role in the ceremonies.

Parenthetically, there is also a tradition that the Stone of Destiny was moved to Scotland, and ended up as the coronation stone in Westminster Abbey in England.

Another Temhair

For the sake of completeness, and to illustrate that the Atlantis story will not fit "any old pile of stones", we will now visit another "Temhair." Although almost all the existing literature says that Tara was the site of the supreme king, there are those who raise objections. One argument is based on the geographic information from Claudios Ptolemaios, from about 140 AD. It is thus several centuries older than the first written evidence from Ireland itself. According to his information, there are two "Regia" on Ireland, two capitals. One is located by present-day Armagh in Northern Ireland, according to a book by Fr. Tom O'Connor, *Turoe & Athenry: Ancient Capitals of Celtic Ireland* (2003), summarized by Dr. Kieran Jordan on the Internet. The other could be Turoe, where the finest decorated Iron Age stone on Ireland is found.

Turoe and Tara have the same name in Gaelic, i.e., Temhair (Temair). Ptolemaios called the southern Regia REGIA ETERA (only capitals existed in those days). The dative of Temhair is "i Temhra", which is reasonably close to Ptolemaios' ETERA.

Near the Turoe stone, which is standing on a hill, there is a village name "Knocknadala", originally "Cnoc na Dail", which means something like 'hill of the great assembly'. No other place on Ireland supposedly has this name. It has been suggested to indicate that this was the capital of the whole island.

The place appears in an old Irish document, "Dindsenchas" from Carn Conaill (near Athenry, between Galway and Turoe). It tells of how the Fir Bolg people conquered that part of Ireland and constructed an "oppidium" unit there (a fortified small town on a high location, in the Hallstatt and La Tène tradition). Local folklore in Kiltullagh (Athenry, Co. Galway) says that the area there called Cotiny (Carrowkeel) once was a part of an ancient town. According to Dr. Jordan, this could be the capital of the Fir Bolg, while the previous inhabitants, Cruithin, had their capital in present Northern Ireland. These would be the two cities by the name Regia on Ptolemaios' map: Knocknadala and Armagh, respectively.

Those who claim that the southern Regia was the political centre of Ireland, argue that ancient sources indicate that the most important harbour anywhere on the British Islands was on the Irish west coast. Even Ptolemaios mentioned that there was only one important

© William Finnerty

The stone at Turoe. It is in La Tène-stile from the Early Iron Age, and is assumed to date from 200 BC ± 50 years.

Ptolemaios' "Hibernia" around 140 AD. He used the wrong dimension for Earth, so his data have here been fitted to a modern map by using the two "Regia" as reference. Triangels are headlands, circles are river mouths, and squares are towns. Dots along the coast are joined by a straight line.

town on the west coast, but on the other hand, it was a world harbour that all sailors visited. Those who argue for Turoe's importance claim that Ptolemaios was talking about Clarinbridge, located just to the southeast of present-day Galway. However, Ptolemaios map gives a different picture. The one and only town on the west coast, Magnata, ends up precisely at Sligo.

On the rest of the island there are only two towns by the sea, Eblana and Manapia. One could suspect that they were located near present-day Dundalk and Dublin, respectively. The river between them, Oboca, could in that case be the Boyne. In the inland in that region there are two towns: Dunum and Laberus. The island apparently has its name from a southerly town, Hibernis. But where is Tara?

We can get inspiration from another continent, from the Hittite Kingdom in Anatolia about 3,500 years ago. I quote from a clay tablet with cuneiform script in the Hittite language: "The land belongs to the Storm God alone! Heaven, earth and the people belong to the Storm God alone! He has made Labarna, the king, his administrator and given all of Hatti to him. Labarna will continue to administer all of this land with his hand. May the Storm God destroy whomever may approach Labarna's person, [unreadable], and the borders." (IBoT 1.30:2-8)

It has been concluded that Labarna was the first king, but judging from the quote, Labarna could alternatively be the supreme king. Compare with the city on Hibernia, "Laberus". An unstressed syllable *-er- in Indo-European, was changed to -ar- in Germanic languages. Perhaps the same applies for the Hittite language, especially considering that those two language branches have been said to be close to one another. If so, then the town Laberus literally might be "Laberna's town", meaning the town of the supreme king—exactly what Irish mythology claims that Tara was.

It seems more plausible that Tara and Sligo were the number one and two in the Irish hierarchy of regional centres, and that the two Regias shared the third position in Ptolemaios' time. Tara with the Boyne Valley may well have been the political and religious centre, while Sligo most likely was the centre for trade, with its big harbour.

Obviously, Turoe has no interest for our discussion on Atlantis.

It is also of interest to note that Ptolemaios' geographical information was more in error than Plato's information about the length and width. This is yet another argument why it is less likely that he got the geographic information from contemporary travellers.

4: Orichalcum

There is an enigma in Plato's story: *From the earth they dug out whatever was to be found there, solid as well as fusile, and that which is now only a name and was then something more than a name—orichalcum—was dug out of the earth in many parts of the island, being more precious in those days than anything except gold.*

Exactly what is orichalcum (or orichalkos as Plato probably spelled it)? In Modern Greek, "orichalkos" means 'brass', but brass was not invented in the Stone Age—though they did have copper in modest amounts. Besides, brass cannot be dug out from the earth. The word "chalkos" by itself means bronze. "Ori" itself means 'rock', 'mountain'.

When it comes to the use of orichalcum, Plato mentioned that the wall around the citadel "flashed with the red light of orichalcum". Concerning Poseidon's temple, he wrote that "all other parts, columns and walls and floor, they covered with orichalcum". The pillar that the law was written on was "by orichalcum", though.

A Red Substance

In this chapter I will speculate rather freely around some alternative hypotheses. The first idea is that "orichalcum" shall be translated 'ochre', notably the red variant—that is, burnt ochre. The word "ochre" comes from a Greek word for pale, as it has a pale yellow colour. The mineral is an iron hydrate (the same as in rust, but the colour is much paler). When burnt (i.e., heated) the water disappears, and it gets a dark red colour. The mineral is now Fe_2O_3, hematite (literally 'bloodstone', which suggests its colour). It was very common during the Neolithic to strew red ochre in graves, all over Europe, from northern Scandinavia in the north and to the Urals in the east.

The first objection to this interpretation of orichalcum is that ochre was known to Plato. It is called ochra in Modern Greek, and since it comes from a verb for 'making pale', it apparently refers to yellow (raw) ochre—a common house colour in Athens.

The English word "chalk" (Germanic "kalk") supposedly comes from Latin "calx" and refers to the product when one heats up calcium carbonate. The word has been used for various solid substances that result when heating other solid substances. It is of course the same root as Greek "chalkos", 'bronze' (today it has also taken the meaning 'copper', but the original word for copper is "kypros").

How would one then form a word for 'burnt ochre' in Greek? Perhaps by combining "ochra + chalkos" into "ochrichalkos", and abbreviating to "orichalkos"? If this is the correct interpretation of the word orichalkos, then the temples were beautifully and intensely red—like the red cottages on the Swedish countryside, that mainly get their colour from iron oxide. It is basically rust. If that was the most valuable thing next to gold in the days of Atlantis, I am not sure whether to laugh or cry...

A problem with this interpretation is that the pillar with the law on was "*of* orichalcum". Burnt ochre is a dye; one cannot make a pillar out of it.

Copper, on the other hand, can both be used for making a pillar (it's also very suitable for engraving, why virtually all outdoor plaques to this day are made of copper), and it can be used to cover other surfaces (as sheet metal). Metallic copper does occur sparingly in nature, though apparently not on Ireland. The colour is reddish, and it has a flashy reflection unlike burnt ochre. Furthermore, copper was known during the Neolithic, and Plato did not mention copper in the dialogues.

But if orichalcum was copper, then why did not Plato call it "chalkos" (its modern name) or "kypros" or similar—the old Greek word cognate to "copper"?

A Paradox

There is a paradox in all this, that I so far have neglected: Plato knew the word orichalkos, but not its meaning, at the same time as it was supposedly translated from Egyptian. How can one translate something one does not understand?

There are a few logical possibilities:

1: The meaning of the word was known to Solon but not to Plato. Hardly likely.

2: The story does not come from Egypt, but from a Greek or at least Indo-European tradition, and thus no translation took place. Alas, this argument does not hold, because the name of Atlas' younger twin was given in both Greek and "Atlantic" (Eumelos and Gadeiros, respectively).

3: The Egyptian word was translated literally, part by part ("ori-chalkos", 'ore-bronze'). This alternative is very logical.

This is what could have happened: Copper was found

in nature as ore. Later it was discovered how to make the alloy bronze, by smelting it together with tin. Since a solid that is produced by heating another solid is called chalkos, that became the Greek name of bronze. Thus, it appears logical that orichalkos could mean "the naturally occurring substance in bronze"—which is copper.

There is actually one more argument that can be made. Cyprus is often said to be named after the Greek word for copper: Kypros. The same can be said about Ireland, since Hibernia apparently is cognate to Kypros; and so is, by extension, Iberia. Both Ireland and Eire are obviously derived from the old name Hibernia. Can we test it? I suggest looking for old copper mines near the (ancient) Irish town of Hibernis. Well guess what, of five major copper mining locations in Early Bronze Age Ireland, four are located near that town.

An idea perhaps worth considering, is that "orichalcum" could have been the original word for the metal copper. The word "copper" is traditionally thought to have come from the name of the island Cyprus, but what if it really came from the town Hibernis, being a trade name for their processed copper ore? That would also explain how the name Atlantis could have been forgotten, and replaced with the name Hibernia.

Eire is really the copper island. Next time you hear someone talk about Ireland as a green island, remember that it is also green from verdigris, the product of copper and old age.

Speaking of verdigris, did I mention that they slaughtered an ox so that the blood ran over the pillar of orichalcum? Blood contains haemoglobin, which takes up oxygen. Perhaps, then, the point was to remove the verdigris from the inscription. Plato did mention that they cleaned the inscriptions after pouring the blood on them. It is possible, I guess, that the purpose was initially completely practical, and not that the blood had any religious significance. For later sailors, though, sacrificing a ram over the totem in the prow of the ship was a religious act.

A Long Shot

There is a possibility, which is controversial since it contradicts the prevailing view among archaeologists: That orichalcum could have been iron. Supposedly, iron was not known on Ireland during the Stone Age. However, we have the following to consider: First, in the fill material in the 6-stadia diameter ditch-and-dike at Tara, waste from iron manufacture was found. Since the rest of the construction is from the Stone Age, and since the dike fits into the picture of the general architecture, one might assume that the bank, too, would be from the Stone Age—if it were not for the iron manufacturing. However, what if they actually knew about iron manufacture? It is a long shot, but without dating the dike in some absolute way, the possibility cannot be ruled out.

Second, iron is the metal in ochre. Iron could have been discovered by chance when making ochre, so if ochre is a possible interpretation of the word, then so is iron.

Third, one of the earliest finds of iron implements was made in Alacahöyük (also written Alaca Hüyük in the literature) in northern central Turkey. Thirteen very rich graves from the mid third millennium BC have been found there (Mellaart, 1978). The graves were built as rectangular chambers under mounds. They had timber roofs, and timber or stone slabs for sides. Their size was up to 6 - 8 m long and 1 m deep. Amber was found, gold, bronze, copper—and two iron daggers with gold inlays. In the early days—although later than this—iron was many times more valuable than gold in the Middle East.

Now, the description of the graves matches rather well the contemporary graves of the Funnel Beaker Culture of northern Europe and the southwest Baltic Sea. Amber is only found within the area of that cultural group. They were the megalith builders of northern Europe, and thus, according to the hypothesis, formed part of the Atlantic Empire. Thus, there is reason to suspect that people from the Atlantic Empire, of Central Europe, have settled in a fortified city in Anatolia. Since some of the world's oldest iron implements were found there, one must keep an open mind to the possibility that the Atlanteans knew about iron manufacture very early on.

The sceptic will then ask, "Why haven't we found out about that before?" One possible reason could be that it was kept a secret for millennia. Perhaps it was only performed inside that ditch and dike at Tara. It may have been an almost "religious" secret, well kept. Many myths from different regions tell us that early metal making was kept a secret; myths from as diverse places as Egypt, Greece, and Finland, just to mention a few.

Others may ask, "Why don't we find more iron in tombs?" There may be several good reasons for that. First, during the time of the Trojan War, iron was only used for agricultural purposes, not for weapons, according to Homer. Thus, it is not likely to ever have been put in a grave (I suppose those two daggers are the exceptions that prove the rule, as they say). Second, there are indications of a tradition of returning the metal to nature after its use. If ochre from mires were used, the iron implements may have been deposited in the mire again, where they may have disappeared completely by now. Perhaps they had a better sense of "sustainable development" than we do.

In essence, until that dike at Tara with the traces of iron making has been dated, we cannot completely rule out that Atlantis was first with iron making, or that orichalcum meant iron. If so, then iron might even have been before copper on Ireland, and it may have been iron that gave Atlantis its technological "cutting edge"— figuratively speaking, because they apparently preferred flint for weapons (or better still, porcellanite from Tievebulliagh or Rathlin Island).

For the time being, copper seems the safest bet, but I am not through yet. Now that we have identified Poseidon's temple, we know from archaeology that there was quartz on it. Could orichalcum be quartz?

A Final Thought

The argument could go like this: Assume that "chalcum" really means 'chalk', its cognate word. In Denmark, for instance, they distinguish between soft and hard rock. The soft rock in Denmark is largely chalk, the hard rock igneous rocks such as granite—in which quartz may be found. The first word in orichalcum, "ori", a cognate to English 'ore', means rock. Thus, orichalcum might actually mean 'hard-rock chalk', as opposed to regular soft chalk. When crystalline, quartz looks similar to diamond (albeit with a different crystal shape), but when opaque, it is white and bright as chalk.

If orichalcum was indeed quartz, then Newgrange

might have been restored pretty well now. Of course, Plato wrote that Poseidon's Temple was covered with silver, while on Newgrange they found quartz. Another long shot association that can be made, is that silver was mined from the quartzite near Simrishamn in southern Sweden in ancient times. It is found together with lead there. Near the quarries, there are rock carvings from the megalith culture (such as the one on the book cover).

Could orichalcum have been lead? some might ask. Lead has been known since ancient times, together with gold, silver, and copper—but it is not red, no more than quartz is. The counter-argument could be that Plato associated to a copper alloy when writing, and invented the colour himself, so to say.

Incidentally, the quartz found at Newgrange was lying around its base, as it still is at Knowth. Poseidon's Palace did therefore probably not look like the picture on the back cover of this book during its Atlantic heydays.

Speaking of that picture, what does it look like? Consider also the pillar-like stone outside the entrance, which threw a shadow into the passage. With that as a phallic symbol, the mound itself clearly resembles the belly of a pregnant Mother Earth, with a passage (vagina) leading in to a chamber (the womb). It is easy to see the fertility symbolism—the similarity is too obvious to miss.

Conclusion

Several possibilities have been presented, and in the literature there are many more. One could add other potential candidates, such as rock carvings, platinum (as suggested by Felici Vinci in *Omero nel Baltico*), or perhaps meteoritic iron, which does not rust. However, I will just leave the question at this—a few suggestions with some accompanying arguments, and definitely without claiming to have found the answer.

Hopefully, having come up with a strong candidate for the location of Atlantis, archaeologists and linguists might be able to combine their expertise and come up with a more definite answer—unless, of course, Plato invented "orichalcum". The interpretation of the word depends on its history, so without knowing anything about Atlantis, it would be virtually impossible to understand it.

Maybe you wonder which of these I believe in? Let me answer with a story. When my grandfather was standing at the helm of a whale ship in the South Atlantic Ocean around 1920, the captain pointed out some icebergs up ahead, and asked him what he intended to do. He started answering with the words "I believe..." whereupon the captain abruptly interrupted him and said, "It will do you no good to *believe*, you have to *know*!"

The same can be said about orichalcum—it is no point in believing in one explanation or the other. As long as we do not know, we have to keep all possible options open. Just as when sailing among icebergs.

In this chapter it has been demonstrated how easy it is to make a falsehood seem believable. Although each of the presented hypotheses might seem plausible, they are all wrong—with the possible exception of one of them. It is easy to get lost on "stepping stones" of false etymology.

After issuing this warning, I will endeavour to suggest some more speculative connections in the next chapter. Keep in mind that until tested and proven, all ideas are to be viewed with healthy scepticism.

5. To Think Free is Great

The motto on Uppsala University in Sweden reads, "To think free is great, to think right is greater." However, most visitors today interpret "to think right" as 'not to think for oneself', and they thus feel the motto ought to read, "To think right is great, to think free is greater." Let us by all means think freely, while remaining self-critical. In this spirit, I want to ventilate some non-orthodox ideas that are related to the interpretation of Atlantis.

Let me sum up first. We have concluded that the story told by Plato contains the memory of:

1) The former island of Dogger Bank that sunk in the North Sea around 6,100 BC as a result of the Storegga Slide, possibly in combination with the catastrophic drainage of glacial Lake Agassiz in Canada;

2) The fact that elephants—what is now called mammoths—lived on that island;

3) The general geography of the island Ireland;

4) Two of the three large passage tombs of the Boyne Valley;

5) Several characteristic elements of Tara.

Thus, the tale is apparently a mix-up, with elements from different times and places: Dogger Island in the

7th millennium BC, and Ireland in the fourth millennium BC. Contamination of the tale with elements from different times seems to be the rule rather than the exception. Consequently, we have to expect that also the main remaining element—the war with Athens—could be from another time, notably younger. When a fleet attacked the Eastern Mediterranean, the older topos of Atlantis may have been attached to them for one reason or another. It does not necessarily mean that they were from the island Atlantis, nor from the Atlantic Empire, nor indeed from the area of the Atlantic Empire—although if they were not, we have to come up with some other plausible explanation of why they were mistaken for Atlanteans.

The Neolithic ®evolution

What we want to know is, of course, what other information in Plato's dialogues is useable. Take the fact that Athens allegedly saved the peoples of the Eastern Mediterranean from slavery. Does that mean that Atlantis had a system of slavery, or is that a contamination? Well, there is one way of testing for this: DNA. If they took slaves, then DNA from populations living around them ought to show up in their gene pool primarily among women, and not among men. Why? Because women are abducted more frequently than men are in war; taken as concubines while the men are slaughtered. In addition, even if both sexes were taken, female slaves are far more likely than male to produce offspring. If you do not believe me, remember how (in the Argonautica) Hypsipyle and the other women of Lemnos had killed all their men, since they were too fond of their captive women, caring more for their bastard children

72

than those by their lawful wives. If you prefer modern medical data rather than myth for argument, check out the ancestry of the inhabitants in Belém, Brazil; they are to about 50% descendents of Native American women, but only to 5% of Native American men. This demonstrates that women of low social groups, and men of high social groups, are most likely to produce offspring, relatively speaking.

In a forthcoming book about DNA, *European DNA from a Geographer's Perspective*, I am analysing a large number of DNA data from Europe, compiled from the literature. It involves both mtDNA (mitochondrial DNA, inherited from the mother) and the Y chromosome (inherited from father to sons). The result in this respect is that Western Europe has far more female than male DNA from the Middle East. Furthermore, the frequencies in general seem higher in the megalithic core areas than in other areas. Most notably, though, over one hundred individuals from actual megalithic tombs in the Basque provinces of Spain have been analyzed for mtDNA, and they have significantly more Middle East-ancestry than the present Basque population. In fact, more than any European population has today. The closest today is northern Portugal—a core megalith area.

Thus, DNA data seems to lend strong support to the idea that they did take slaves from the Eastern Mediterranean area. This raises another interesting topic. The gene types in question, the "haplotypes" as the geneticists call them, have been rather convincingly correlated with the advent of agriculture to Western Europe. Now, if the genes came with slaves, the inevitable conclusion is that agriculture, too, came with slaves. That amounts to a completely new idea and proposition, and something that would turn many attempts at interpretation upside down. Nevertheless, it is very plausible, since it offers a straightforward explanation for why it took several millennia for agriculture to go from "fringe" to "mainstream". All novelties diffuse faster from top to bottom in society, than the reverse.

Incidentally, I fail to see how something that took several thousand years can be called a revolution. The term is well established, though, which is why I in irony spelled it the "Neolithic ®evolution".

The American Connection

Speaking of mtDNA, there is one haplogroup that is especially interesting in relation to Atlantis: X. As you recall, the story says that the Atlantic Ocean was surrounded by a continent on the opposite side. How could they have known that if they did not go there? Furthermore, if they did go there, perhaps they left some trace in the form of DNA. Apparently, that is just what they did. North American Indian tribes, all over the continent (but not in South America) have in average 3% of mtDNA-haplotype X. It exists in Europe, but not in Asia. The highest frequencies have been found in Druze, a Muslim religious sect in southern Lebanon and adjacent areas, which migrated there from Egypt in 1017 AD. However, the second highest frequency was found among the Etruscans, and the third on the Orkney Islands.

It seems very probable that somebody sailed across the Atlantic Ocean, sometime long before the Vikings.

Haplogroup X is old in Europe, but it only occurs in low frequencies; the average frequency in Europe is about the same as that in North America. Curiously, it is

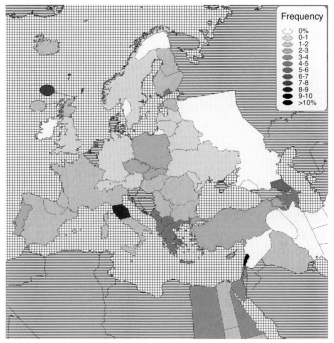

The frequency of mtDNA-haplogroup X was highest in the Druze sample (27%), followed by Toscana (8.3%) and Orkney (7.2%). Those three populations may reveal something about the ancient DNA-distribution of the Phoenicians, Etruscans, and Atlanteans, respectively. (The ovals north of Ireland represent the frequency on Orkney and the Western Islands.)

rare on Ireland. The low frequency there suggests that it may not have been the inhabitants on the main island that did the sailing, but rather those on the northern islands—which, of course, is the direction to America if one follows the easiest route, the one over Iceland and Greenland. We do not know for sure where the Phoenicians came from, but O'Brien (1834, p. 415) illustrated the similarity of the Irish language with the Phoenician using an example (he failed to give credits, though). Plautus quoted the Phoenician leader Hanno as

The pineapple plant looks like a flower in the wide sense of the word, and the flower itself (in the strict sense) does not fall off when the fruit grows out. Homer referred to the Lotus-eaters as those who ate flowers.

saying in his tongue: "Nith al o nim, ua lonuth secorat-hessi ma com syth." Compare with the Irish translation: "An iath al a nim, uaillonac socruidd se me com sit." The Phoenician language we know was Semitic, though.

Another theoretical possibility would be that the transatlantic voyages were even earlier—before Dogger Bank sank in the cold sea. The tsunami from the Storegga slide could have destroyed all harbours and ships used in the voyages, and thus put a sudden end to it. Only some tales would survive.

Such journeys—regardless of when they took place— would explain why some features in, e.g., the Odyssey, appear influenced by American realities. I am thinking of the Lotus-eaters, who, in my opinion, may have been pineapple-cultivators in the Caribbean Sea (pineapple has been cultivated there for about ten thousand years, and also much later navigators have had trouble getting their crews to leave tropical island paradises).

Since women were brought from Europe to America, we either have to assume a colony established from Europe, or that Native Americans sailed to Europe and brought women home with them. The fact that the memory survives in Europe speaks for the former alternative, but the fact that only female genes have been identified from the migration speaks for the latter.

The concentration of the X haplogroup on the Orkneys reminds me of the Irish myth of the Fomorians: Giants and pirates that were expelled to the northern sea after having ruled Ireland for a while. They were in fact the original inhabitants of Ireland, we are told. Although, perhaps the myth really spoke of Dogger Bank.

The end of the Ice Age brought large-scale flooding to southeastern North America and the Caribbean region. During the Ice Age, that region would have been a very good place for human habitation. There was a window of opportunity for transatlantic cultural exchange during a few thousand years after the Ice Age. After that, rising sea levels and a changing climate may have undermined the American civilisation, and natural disasters may have destroyed the infrastructure for communication. The ultimate demise of transatlantic journeys could have been the event of 6,100 BC that flooded Dogger Bank.

Although this is very speculative, it does not seem impossible that an early advanced culture in northwestern Europe, a "proto-Atlantis", really was destroyed when their island was swallowed by the sea over eight thousand years ago. Thousands of years later, a new civilisation (without defining the word) had emerged, and most of the myth refers to that later "classic Atlantis". Perhaps, though, they deliberately copied things from proto-Atlantis, such as the concentric lakes.

It seems that classic Atlantis had an almost Viking-style society, with elements such as barter, slavery, long journeys at sea, and the rule of law at home. They even seem to have had some form of union; a united kingdom that in a way amounted to a combination of the first European Union, and the first North Atlantic Treaty Organization.

Why, then, would a culture that had existed for so long, go under some time before historic times? Plato told us about the war, and how Athens defeated Atlantis. In my next book on this topic, I will discuss that war. It is a long story, but one that Plato never got around to. Came to think of it, I am now stopping at the same point where he stopped. Since I know what the continuation is, I think I understand why he stopped where he did. My reason is, that the continuation requires a thorough pre-sentation of the Eastern Mediterranean prehistory, and that is no small task. Could it be that Plato realized the same thing?

As for the detailed geography of Atlantis, that will have to wait, too. Many pieces in the puzzle of European prehistory will have to be re-examined first. One being the origin of the Indo-European languages. Hardly any-thing suggests that it came from Atlantis. In fact, there is more reason to suspect that Basque was the *lingua franca* of the Atlantic Empire. Before you go "Yes! I knew it!" let me remind you, it is nothing more than a hunch on my part at this stage.

For more background on the culture and people on the Atlantic sea-shore of Europe and northern Africa, I suggest reading *Facing the Ocean: The Atlantic and Its Peoples 8000 BC-AD 1500* (Cunliffe, 2001). Note that the area covered essentially agrees with the core megalith area, and thus, the peoples described might be related to the old Atlanteans. However, as is often the case in compilations of that kind, data from the older periods and from other branches of science are less well researched. It excels only in periods after the one of interest for us. A detail worth noting, though, is that stories of sunken cities exist in many places along the Atlantic sea shore.

There is no lack of leads for starting to disentangle the rope, so to say. For instance, "Cleito" means the 'illustrious'. One translation to Swedish of that is 'frejdad'. In the Nordic divine mythology, there is a brother and sister called Frej ('Frey') and Freja, who were in charge of fertility (and after whom Friday is named). Their father was Njord, the sea god, who was from the Vaner's stock, not the Aesir's (the Vikings considered the Aesir—a word cognate to Asia—of the Asatro as somehow superior to the other race of gods, the Vaner). In Nordic mythology, Njord was married to Skade, of the giants' race, with blond hair. Tacitus called Scandinavia "Scadinauia", which means 'Skade's Island'. Njord is cognate to Nerthus, a fertility goddess mentioned by Tacitus in "Germanica". Nerthus seems cognate to Nereus, the old man of the sea in Greek mythology, whose daughters the Nereids were. As mentioned earlier, the Nereids stood statue in Poseidon's palace on Atlantis. It seems that we are on track to the Atlantic religion here, but also the Irish; Njord is apparently identical to Manannan mac Lir.

Mythology, archaeology, and genetic data complement each other, and within the near future, after the rediscovery of Atlantis, a new image of the prehistory may emerge. My guess is that the Vaner were the ruling class of the Atlantic Empire, and in fact identical to the Thuata de Danaan (literally 'people of Danaan'; see also page 50), as well as to the Danes, who in Danish mythology conquered the eastern islands from a homeland in southern Scandinavia. Maybe, to stretch the speculation, rivers such as Danaper and the Danube might be named after them.

They could also be related to the Danaids of Greek mythology, that is, the fifty daughters of Danaos (we note the number, and remember how many Nereids there were; furthermore, they had 50 male cousins, 49 of whom they murdered on the wedding night—which reminds me that there are 99 lunations in a Great Year, according to Irish author Robert Graves in *The Greek Myths*). Finally, since the Danaids supposedly introduced Demeter's mystery to Eleusis and Greece, that mystery might ultimately be derived from Atlantis and the Mansion of Boyne (O'Brien, 1834, p. 351, suggested that Newgrange was a Mithratic temple). The secrecy of the ancient mysteries was never broken, why we hardly know anything about them. However, we do know that phantoms were part of the Eleusinian mysteries, and that they were celebrated at the night of September 28th – 29th.

Is there a connection with Halloween? The differing dates might be the result of using different calendars through a few thousand years. Rather than making skulls of pumpkins, perhaps the megalith people simply used the real stuff from the graves. Perhaps priests would pretend that the dead still lived on, albeit as phantoms. It sure would explain a lot of the mythology and folklore in Europe. Of course, this is pure speculation, which I am mentioning only to illustrate how one might make new connections—connections that would have been excessively far fetched if we had not had reason to believe Atlantis was megalith Ireland.

Ale's Stones

As a final comment, I will return to the measurement system of Atlantis. It is not a simple thing to measure an island of Ireland's size with 3% precision. One may also wonder, how come that the size of the island could be given with such precision, even if only one significant digit was used? Perhaps the length of the yard intentionally was designed to fit the size of the island, just as the nautical mile and the metre were created by sub-dividing the Earth's dimensions. Consider this; a stadium would then be defined as $1/3,000^{th}$ of the island's length, or $1/2,000^{th}$ of its width, while a yard is $1/200^{th}$ of a stadium, and an ell is $1/300^{th}$ of a stadium. However, we can not know if they actually did define the yard in that way—the correspondence might also be a coincidence.

Students of the megalithic yard have claimed that it was in use roughly from 3,000 BC and for at least 1,500 years in monumental constructions. If it were true that it only existed towards the end of the megalithic era, then it would be reasonable to see it as the culmination of the Stone Age science and development. A common measurement system is essential for trade. This system might have been instrumental for the cultural bloom of the Bronze Age, one might speculate.

What made me accept the controversial idea of a megalithic unit was that I found it in a Scandinavian

Ale's Stones, the stone "ship" at Kåseberga, southernmost Sweden. The four stones along the length axis are of Cambrian quartzite, the rock in which silver was once mined. They have been transported many kilometres.

monument: Ale's Stones (*Ale* or *Ales Stenar* in Swedish). It is located within the megalithic area in southernmost Scandinavia, but archaeologists believe it to be from about 400 AD. The standing stones have their length axis in about 135°, corresponding to the local midwinter-sunrise and midsummer-sunset direction. Curt Roslund, Professor in Astronomy, has calculated that the stones —unlike all other similar monuments in Sweden, which are from the Viking Age—are constructed as two opposing hyperbolas. The distance between the stones along the axis, the *latus rectum*, is 2.23 ±0.08 m. When laying out the design the old-fashioned way, with a base line, pins and a measuring line, the smallest unit needed is 1/4 *latus rectum*, or about 0.557 m. This is statistically identical to the megalithic ell of 0.553 m, calculated from monuments of known megalithic age in Western Europe.

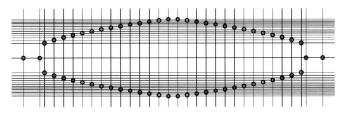

Idealized geometry of Ale's Stones. The four stones on the central axis are of quartzite, and their orientation is 135.08° ±0.04° (my measurement). The distance between the other stones along that axis is the so-called latus rectum, which in this case is equal to 4 megalithic ell, or 2.23 metres. Their construction axis is about 135.32°, as calculated by Roslund (1993). The monument is located at latitude N 55°22.951', elevation about 37 metres.

One may thus suspect, that the megalithic ell was the basic measurement unit when they built Ale's Stones. While the yard was the basic unit in Britain, the ell was the basic unit in Sweden until the metric system was adopted. The national reference, a wooden stick, is located in Rydaholm in Småland. The fact that it is made of wood means that it can change length, and the same thing apparently happened to the megalithic measurement system.

A Swedish foot is shorter than the British is, but longer than the megalithic. The Danish is longer than all those. Neither the Danish nor the Swedish unit matches the dimensions of the monument Ale's Stones, nor the British for that matter, but the megalithic one does perfectly as we have seen. However, in parts of Germany the foot still has the same length as the megalithic one.

It sure seems like there was one system from the beginning, but that the local references (once created from the same original reference) have changed length with time. The length of the foot in various places is given here:

Russia	356 mm	Flandria	343 mm	Prussia	333 mm
Denmark	314 mm	England	305 mm	Sweden	297 mm
Leipzig	282 mm	Frankfurt	274 mm	Megalith	276 mm

I must credit the students of the megalithic measurement system for bringing to my attention that northwestern Europe might have produced an advanced culture already during the Neolithic. However, the existence of a megalithic measurement system is far from universally accepted. Some scholars dismiss it with statements such as "Accounts of a megalithic yard are science fiction". I do not want to embarrass the person who wrote those words by mentioning his name. However, I found that the four length values he himself gave in the same paper, could be shown statistically to correspond to a megalithic foot as design unit (in Moravia, Czech Republic). The method is simple when you have access to several values: Check if the mean and standard deviation of the remainder differ significantly from the result when using a distance unit chosen at random.

Ingenious new ideas may be wrong, or they may be right; we will never know which, unless we stick strictly to the scientific method. This applies equally to both sides of a scientific debate. Hypotheses must be formulated and tested properly, without irrelevant arguments. Every person—scholar or amateur—who makes an effort, deserves to be taken seriously as long as (s)he adheres to the rules of the scientific method (which I have not done strictly in this book, since it is not a scientific article, mind you). You may think that something is science fiction, but keep that to yourself—instead, show with valid and relevant arguments why it is not correct, and treat your colleagues with respect. That is the way to advance science.

This said, it is clear that there really are many nonsensical ideas out there today, and I can understand why scientists short of time dismiss most of them without even trying to evaluate them. Resources are limited. But the megalithic yard seems to be an idea worth studying.

Amazingly, those who live in the U.S. or parts of Central America are still using this stone-age measurement system. It is called the Imperial measurement system, with the British Empire in mind, although as it turns out it probably comes from the Atlantic Empire (and is surviving today in the "American Empire").

The system is good if you use fractions in your mathematics. That is what everyone did before the Arabs invented the zero. One could say that the Irish understood many things, but the Arabs understood nothing. That is not insignificant; someone actually wrote a doctor thesis about the Russian word for 'nothing' ("nitchevo"), a word with well over a hundred different meanings. So be forewarned: *nothing* really matters!

6. On Myth and Science

$\mathfrak{A}$ tlantis is now effectively a myth, but the origin of the myth was the two dialogues by Plato. The story only started catching people's imagination during the last few centuries. Many contemporaries of Plato, such as Aristotle, considered it pure fiction. Then again, they did not believe in Pytheas either (the Greek who sailed to Ultima Thule). In this enlightened day and age we are better able to distinguish fact from fiction, though. Or are we?

There are many reasons why we might end up holding erroneous beliefs. Let us start with a brief look at the nature of science, before continuing with more philosophical speculations around the Atlantis myth. Little will it surprise me if humanist scholars will criticize this chapter; alas, after my criticism of their blunders in geography through the millennia, that should not be begrudged them.

The scientific method for empirical sciences that is most widely accepted, is the hypothetical-deductive method. It consists of making observations, explaining the observations in terms of a hypothesis, deducing logical consequences of it, and testing in an attempt to prove the hypothesis wrong. If it fails the test it is thrown out, but for every test it passes it is strengthened, and eventually elevated to theory. Note that what scientists call hypotheses, laymen call theories, and what scientists call theories, laymen call scientific facts or laws of nature.

In this manner, theory is laid on theory like brick upon brick in building a house. However, one day the whole building might collapse if the design was poor, or the foundation was unsound. When this happens in science we are talking about a paradigm shift, after Thomas Kuhn in *The Structure of Scientific Revolutions* (1962). A paradigm can be seen as a shared way of defining a topic or a problem, and an agreement on suitable and acceptable methods to study it: What is relevant and what is not, and what are the criteria for good science? In essence, a paradigm is a set of assumptions.

One should of course always stick to logic. In so doing, one must make oneself aware of ones assumptions, so they can be evaluated. Finally, one must learn to distinguish between relevant and irrelevant arguments. Authorities are irrelevant, for instance. Anyone and everybody can make errors and be wrong.

Let me rephrase that so nobody misses the point: Don't take anybody's word for what Atlantis is or isn't!

Speaking of which, a search for "Atlantis" in an on-line bookstore gave 5,309 hits. Some place Atlantis in America, either north or south. Or maybe in between. Some believe it was a continent that sank in the Atlantic Ocean. Some believe it was Santorini, a small, volcanic island in the Aegean Sea. Some believe it was the Antarctic 10,000 years ago "when it was warm there". Except, it was *not* warm there 10,000 years ago. Introducing a lie in a subordinate clause is a common trick in propaganda, and I have seen it done deliberately even in TV News. Sadly, few Americans realize that theirs is one of the few countries where war propaganda is legal.

Be alert, and analyze the arguments. Also, get used to never accepting a word in an argument if you do not completely understand it. Let me illustrate with an example, using a word that everybody knows: "God".

If you ask Christian believers what exactly "God" is, they might reply, "I don't know". Those same people might tell you that "God created the world", since many in America still believe in the creation. Now, to show you what my point is, combine those two statements and you will get: "I don't know who or what created the world". Evidently a true statement, but it hardly makes us any wiser, does it?

This is why it is pointless to use poorly defined words in an argument or a scientific hypothesis: We cannot build on it. Since we cannot evaluate it, the argument has no value; it is neither true nor false in logical terms. It is that middle case which Jaakko Hintikka described in *The Principles of Mathematics Revisited* (1996). His logic, with three possible cases, is beautiful. Let me summarize his conclusion in laymen's terms: Statements that are neither true nor false are logically rather useless.

The one who wants to avoid believing in nonsense should go to the bottom of things, admit when he does not understand, and insist on an explanation. No one is easier to fool than the one who is afraid of appearing ignorant. The smart man questions where the fool nods.

Science, logic, and the analysis of arguments is not just for scientists; it is for everyone, always—it is the very foundation of our civilisation. Logical analysis is the only way to persuade even oneself. Remember, while it is immature to trust the convictions of others, it is outright foolish to trust the convictions of oneself.

So, what does "science" have to say about Atlantis? It usually avoids the subject. Here is a typical reaction: A professor who read this book commented, that since they could not measure an island the size of Atlantis with any precision during Plato's time, it was even less likely that they could do so during the Stone Age.

What is wrong with this argument? Two things:

First, Plato wrote that they had a high technological level in Atlantis, which was lost because of the disaster. Considering this, the argument above can be rephrased as: "Since they could not measure precisely, Plato must have invented the story; thus, Atlantis did not exist, and consequently, they could not measure precisely." The circle might be an ideal shape in geometry, but not in an argument.

Second, it assumes that development always goes forward—that there are no major setbacks. Other times and cultures do not share this assumption, including Classical Greece. History is also full of examples to the contrary, e.g., the Greek Dark Ages after the Mycenaean civilisation. Thus, the assumption is quite simply invalid.

One reason why we in the western world do not take mythology seriously, might be precisely that this assumption of continuous development is so deeply rooted, that even a scientist uses it by pure habit.

A related assumption that is afflicting research, is that our ancestors were primitive. Objectively this is absurd, yet it is apparently a prejudice held by a majority, possibly even within the academic community. Again, it seems to be peculiar to our culture.

Those who hold these assumptions have no choice but to dismiss the tale of Atlantis, since the tale and the assumptions are mutually exclusive.

Our modern brand of science (and technology, its close cousin) is founded on a strong sense of development optimism, which is intimately related to the notion of continuous development. If development is continuous, there is no room for an early lost civilisation, obviously.

Rather than blaming inexplicable details on the superstition of our ancestors, we should probably suspect our own ignorance, narrow-mindedness and cultural blindness. The poet Karin Boye wrote "Of course it hurts when buds break—why else would Spring hesitate?" The buds that break within us are perhaps our narrow-minded worldviews. But why are we blind?

We all have moral values, and we judge actions against them. However, in the last century philosophers have started questioning whether there is such a thing as universal moral values.

A logical analysis that I made based on the axiom of the survival of the fittest*, showed that the optimal set of moral values will depend on the group's survival strategy. The optimal survival strategy, in turn, depends on the limiting (i.e., hardest) challenges that they face. The two extremes are groups that face widespread natural hazards that can be mitigated effectively, and those that face local, lethal, violent hazards that cannot be mitigated.

The first situation favours a knowledge-intensive and highly structured society, with a legal code, and an unselfish moral. The second would tend to favour a selfish

---

* "The survival of the fittest" is typically called a theory, but in my opinion it is evidently true and impossible to prove—the exact criteria given by Aristotle for an axiom.

strategy where opportunism is the guiding principle for human behaviour—albeit tacitly, since admitting to it would probably be counter-productive. The moral code will likely become "the end justifies the means", diametrically opposite to the first society.

The point is, that coming from one background, it can be hard to guess how people think—and thus to understand their behaviour—in another culture. If this is true in our own time, it is probably the case when studying past cultures as well. Especially if the challenges those cultures faced, in the form of climatic fluctuations and natural hazards, were different (and certainly if those challenges are unknown to us).

Do you know what the real myth is?

Take a few steps back and look at our times. What is our civilisation based on? It is based on the large-scale exploitation of fossil fuel. First coal, now oil. We use it to convert ore to metal, for other manufacturing processes, for transportation, for heating and cooling our buildings, and even for producing food. However, within a few decades to centuries, we will run out of fossil fuel. Since this civilisation is based on an un-sustainable rate of energy consumption, there will be changes. Probably radical changes, and a lower material standard of living.

Furthermore, for the assumption of continuous development to be even remotely credible, the world must be very young. Four to five thousand years or so. Such as it was in the Christian myth of the Creation. Could this downright be the origin of the assumption of continuous development? It is hard not to suspect that we are still influenced by this myth in a modernized form, where the "Creation" has been replaced by the "Neolithic Revolution". Using the word "revolution" for a several thousand years long "evolution", is a hint that there is some sub-conscious element at play.

So you know what the real myth is? The real myth is not Atlantis or Ragnarök or the Trojan War. No, the real myth is that of continuous development. Even the latest invention, sustainable development, is nothing but a slight variation of the continuous-development myth. Denial is another word for it.

Why do modern myths exist? Apparently, it has to do with how the human mind works. We generalize; we simplify in order to bring structure to a complex reality. The generalizations form a set of universal assumptions, of which we are hardly aware. We regard it as evidently true, and do not believe that it needs to be proven. Kind of like an axiom. However, in everyday life, what some people treat as axiom, others call prejudice.

These opinions, to use a more neutral word, are formed in each person based on her experiences. The narrower the field of experience is, the wider is the field that is seen as constant, that will be taken for granted and self-evident. Perhaps it is enlightening to see this as statistics. For each variable where we observe variation, we somehow estimate and store in memory the mean and standard deviation; but a variable in which we see no variation, we treat like a constant instead. A prejudice can then be understood as a variable that is erroneously treated as a constant.

Exactly how the brain works is not yet known, but combining biological and psychological research results, this is how I imagine it might function: Our worldview is expressed as a collection of memories, probabilities, associations and rules. This, I guess, is stored as the physical arrangement of neurons in our brains, in those innumerable connections between the nerve cells. To speed up the thinking—so I imagine—derived facts and conclusions are also stored. Those are the above-mentioned "opinions". Probably their derivations fade away and might be dropped with time.

Eventually, some piece of irrefutable observation might come into direct conflict with one of these derived opinions. When this happens, it takes a lot of energy to re-evaluate the worldview. One can imagine the activity going on in the brain, trying to find new patterns, and re-examining which of the old conclusions are still valid. Outwardly, this phase presents itself as a depression. The person might have dreams that his house is burning, symbolizing how the old construction is destroyed to give place for a new.

Depressions are obviously depressing, why we tend to avoid them. We do that by explaining away any contradictory evidence as long as possible. This includes using the mental mechanism of denial. For instance, people living an energy-consuming life style are likely to filter out information about how limited the oil reserves are. Due to this psychological mechanism, an entire culture can cruise with ever increasing speed towards its own demise. It should not surprise us that past civilisations have succumbed, since anybody with eyes to see can predict where our own is heading.

Another problem lies in the western hectic lifestyle. We have no time for a depression, but we have plenty of doctors ready to prescribe anti-depressive medicines. They might remove the symptoms, but is that good or bad? Do feel-good pills solve the real problems?

Whatever the answer, this cynic might be on the right track: "The only thing we learn from history is that we learn nothing from history." What I mean is that each civilisation seems to be based on some natural resource, that they eventually run out of. Ours is fossil fuel, which we use for many things, including to make fertilizers and multiple our harvests. The Roman Empire exploited the soil around the Mediterranean Sea. Other civilisations have existed for thousands of years based on irrigation, until the soil was destroyed by the salts dissolved in the irrigation water (and the lands remain a desert thousands of years later). Ireland's mountains were fertile agricultural lands too, early in the "Neolithic Revolution", but peat growth destroyed much land.

As you see, the geographic location of Atlantis is just one aspect of the story. An equally intriguing question is why it was forgotten in the first place. In general, why do we loose our history? One answer is natural disasters, but the psychological explanation should also be considered. When the map does not match the reality, too often we tend to hold on to our (mental) map, and turn our eyes away from the reality. Especially if there is something shameful to hide in the real world. An example is the massacre that Sweden carried out in Örkened in Skåne in the year 1678. Majority Swedes still react negatively when that is mentioned, and distortions of the facts (blaming the victims) can be found in the media even after three centuries.

This brings us to another mechanism, namely political and religious propaganda and lies. Myths may be created as narratives for such purposes. Since that same process is active today, understanding how it is done —and why—may help us being more alert to contemporary lies, the most important of which are the ones that are deviously devised in order to start wars. What Plato wrote about Atlantis, "The most important law was not to start war against one another", still holds true.

While some myths were created for political or religious purposes, the ones of most interest are simply tradition handed down through millennia. The task of understanding tradition is fundamentally different from understanding created myth. Because the truth may well be that while the story has been correctly preserved, it is its context that is lost—often its geographic context, as with Atlantis, or its cultural context. First, of course, one has to find out what kind of myth one is dealing with. Then, one has to make oneself aware of any assumptions that one may have, and evaluate them properly.
Motto:

Things are not always what they seem to be.
You have to feel the logic of the words, and
their meaning will change before your eyes.

In all simplicity, this expresses the problem with myth. They can often be interpreted in several ways. An historic myth may be compared to a skipper's story: It seems credible to the one who knows little, incredible to the one who knows more, but it takes inside knowledge to understand that it is true—in another way. Perhaps it is this quality of riddle that makes some stories survive, and not others; they are more interesting, but with time, their true meaning is lost.

Studying the Atlantis myth and its evolution, we can learn fascinating things in many fields. Taken together, it is perhaps the greatest story never told, in spite of the 5,309 hits. This book is but a foreword to the introduction of that story.

References

Bergh, S., 1995: Landscape of the Monuments. A study of the passage tombs in the Cúil Irra region, Co. Sligo, Ireland. *Arkeologiska undersökningar, Skrifter* nr 6: Riksantikvarieämbetet, Sweden.

Collina-Girard, J., 2001: L'Atlantide devant le détroit de Gibraltar ? Mythe et géologie. *Comptes Rendus de l'Académie des Sciences - Series IIA.* 333(4): 233–240.

Cunliffe, B., 2001: *Facing the Ocean: The Atlantic and Its Peoples 8000 BC-AD 1500.* Oxford Press.

Eogan, G., 1987: *Knowth and passage-tombs of Ireland (New Aspects of Antiquity).* Thames & Hudson.

Erlingsson, U., (forthcoming): *European DNA from a Geographer's Perspective.* Lindorm Publishing.

Graves, R., 1955: *The Greek Myths.* Penguin Books.

Hintikka, J., 1996: *The Principles of Mathematics Revisited.* Cambridge University Press.

Kuhn, T., 1962: *The Structure of Scientific Revolutions.* University of Chicago Press.

Mellaart, J., 1978: *The Archaeology of Ancient Turkey.* Rowman & Littlefield.

O'Brien, H., 1834: *The Round Towers of Ireland: The History of the Thuat-de-Danaans.* Parbury and Allen, London.

O'Callaghan, C., 2004: *Newgrange: Temple to Life.* Mercier Press.

O'Connor, T., 2003: *Turoe and Athenry: Ancient Capitals of Celtic Ireland.* Edited by Jordan, K.

O'Kelly, M.J., 1995: *Newgrange: Archaeology, Art and Legend (New Aspects of Antiquity).* Thames & Hudson.

Roslund, C., 1993: EDM Technique Applied to the Prehistoric Monument "Ale's Stones". *Archaeology and Natural Science*, 1: 111-116.

Shephard, A. (ed), 2001: *The Atlantis Dialogue: The Original Story of the Lost Empire.* Excerpts from *Timaeus* and *Critias* by Plato, translated by B. Jowett. Shepard Publications, Los Angeles.

Stout, G. (ed.), 2003: *Newgrange and the bend of the Boyne (Irish Rural Landscapes, V. 1).* Cork University Press.

Thom, A., 1967: *Megalithic Sites in Britain.* Clarendon Press, Oxford, England.

Uistin, L.M., 2000: *Exploring Newgrange.* The O'Brien Press.

Vinci, F., 1998: *Omero nel Baltico.* Fratelli Palombi Editions.

Internet Links

lindorm.com/atlantis
The home site of this book.

www.knowth.com
Photographs, links, book reviews, and links. A good starting point for surfing to the Stone Age. Lists many books on the Boyne Valley sites.

www.carrowkeel.com
Megalithic sites on Ireland, the "Sacred Island" according to the web site name. Contains many interesting facts of a more speculative kind.

www.megalithomania.com
Photographs, accounts of visits.

www.themodernaniquarian.com
A site where guests can post pictures and weblogs, and a lively forum for debate.

www.iol.ie/~sec/sites.htm
A brief guide to megalithic sites on Ireland. Explains the different types of sites in an excellent way.

www.sacredsites.com
Photographs and writings by an anthropologist. Covers over 1000 sites in 80 countries.

www.stonepages.com
Megalithic sites all over Europe, with photographs, folklore, forums, news, and descriptions.

www.theoi.com
A guide to Greek gods, spirits, and monsters.

abob.libs.uga.edu/bobk/phaeth.html
An article analysing the Phaëthon myth as a close comet encounter.

http://fermi.phys.ualberta.ca/~amk/as/aleseng.html
A well-researched article on Ale Stenar.

Indexed Glossary

Term	Page
Aegaeon the hundred-handed one, sea-related god in Homer	39
Aegir Ägir, the sea god in Nordic mythology	39
Aesir Asar, the main race of gods in the Nordic mythology	79
Agassiz, Lake ice dammed lake over Canada during deglaciation	23, 71
Alacahöyük archaeological site in Anatolia, 3rd millennium BC	65
Anatolia the same as Asia Minor, where Turkey is located	58, 66
Argonautica an expedition some decades before the Trojan War	72
Briareus the hundred-handed one, sea-related god in Homer	39
Cairn grave type, a stone mound	31ff, 50ff
Cursus procession road	52
Danaan, Thuata de, the people of the son of the goddess Dana	50, 79
Danaids The 50 daughters of Danaos in Greek mythology	80
Danes People that conquered Denmark and gave name to it	80
Dogger Bank shoal in the North Sea, highest point at 15 m depth	22ff, 71ff
Dolmen grave type: a few standing boulders support one on top	31ff
Empiric based on observation, as opposed to deductive, speculative, etc.	87
Eumelos Greek translation of Gadeiros (see that word)	11, 63
Evenor the father of the Atlantean's earth-born mother Cleito	10, 49, 54
Funnel Beaker Culture Neolithic culture of northern Europe	9, 34, 66
Gadeiros younger twin of Atlas, son of Poseidon and Cleito	11, 63
Gades land near Atlantis and the pillars of Heracles	11
Geomorphology science that studies the landscape and its evolution	4
Heliads daughters of the sun, sisters of Phaëthon in the myth	3
Heracles Hercules, in the Greek form of the name	6ff, 24ff
Hittite early Indo-European civilisation in Anatolia	58
Iberia Spain and Portugal are located on the Iberian Peninsula	24, 64
Jutland Jylland, the mainland peninsula of western Denmark	21

Leucippe the mother of the Atlantean's earth-born mother Cleito   10, 54

Linear B the syllable writing system used in Mycenaean palaces   39

Manannan mac Lir sea god in Irish mythology   5, 39ff, 79

Nereids mermaids, 50 (on Atlantis 100) daughters of Nereus   13, 40, 79ff

Phaëthon illegitimate son of the sun, apparently a meteorite   3ff

Porcellanite mineral, amorphous silica of igneous origin, very hard   67

Poseidon the sea god in Greek mythology   11ff, 39

Ptolemaios, Claudius Greek scientist in Alexandria, d. 165 AD   55ff

Skåne Latin name Scania, the southernmost part of Scandinavia   95

Solon Athenian statesman and poet, initiated democracy 594/593 BC 2, 15, 63

Storegga site of several large submarine slides, the last at 6,100 BC   22, 71, 75

Tholos grave type in Mycenaean Greece, though with few burials   34, 39

Tsunami long-period ocean wave group of seismic origin   5, 22ff, 32, 75

Tyrrhenia the same as the Etruscan area, or Toscana, in present Italy   7ff

Vaner the race of gods in charge of fertility in Nordic mythology   79